Network

www.companionsinchrist.org

So much more!

Companions in Christ offers leaders *so much more* than just printed resources. It offers an ongoing LEADERSHIP NETWORK that provides:

- Opportunities to connect with other churches who are also journeying through *Companions in Christ*
- Helpful leadership tips and articles as well as updated lists of supplemental resources
- Training opportunities that develop and deepen the leadership skills used in formational groups
- A staff available to consult with you to meet the needs of your small group
- An online discussion room where you can share or gather information
- Insights and testimonies from other *Companions in Christ* leaders
- A FREE 48-page *Getting Started Guide* filled with practical tools to help you start a group in your church
- FREE *Companions in Christ* posters to use as you promote the group in your congregation

Just complete this form and drop it in the mail, and you can enjoy the many benefits available to leaders through the *Companions in Christ* NETWORK!

❏ Add my name to the *Companions in Christ* NETWORK <u>email list</u> so that I can receive ongoing information about small-group resources and leadership trainings.

❏ Please send me a FREE 48-page *Getting Started Guide.*

❏ Please send me FREE *Companions in Christ* posters. Indicate quantity needed: _____

Name: _____

Address: _____

City/State/Zip: _____

Church: _____

Email: _____ Phone: _____

ETWLG

MAIL TO: COMPANIONS *in Christ*

UPPER ROOM MINISTRIES
PO BOX 340012
NASHVILLE, TN 37203-9540

The COMPANIONS *in Christ* Series

EXPLORING
the Way

An Introduction to the Spiritual Journey

LEADER'S GUIDE

Marjorie J. Thompson and Stephen D. Bryant

UPPER
ROOM BOOKS®
NASHVILLE

COMPANIONS IN CHRIST
EXPLORING THE WAY: AN INTRODUCTION TO THE SPIRITUAL JOURNEY
Leader's Guide
Copyright © 2005 by Upper Room Books®
All rights reserved.

No part of this book may be reproduced in any manner whatsoever without permission except in the case of brief quotations embodied in critical articles or reviews. For information, write: Upper Room Books®, 1908 Grand Avenue, Nashville, Tennessee 37212.

The Upper Room® Web site http://www.upperroom.org

UPPER ROOM®, UPPER ROOM BOOKS® and design logos are trademarks owned by the Upper Room®, Nashville, Tennessee. All rights reserved.

Unless otherwise stated, scripture quotations are from the New Revised Standard Version Bible, copyright © 1989 by the Division of Christian Education of the National Council of the Churches of Christ in the U.S.A. Used by permission. All rights reserved.

Scripture quotations marked JB are taken from THE JERUSALEM BIBLE, copyright © 1966 by Darton, Longman & Todd, Ltd. and Doubleday, a division of Random House, Inc. Reprinted by permission.

Cover design: Lori Putnam
Cover art: Lori Putnam
Interior icon development: Michael C. McGuire, SettingPace
First printing: 2005

Library of Congress Cataloging-in-Publication
Thompson, Marjorie J., 1953–
    Exploring the way: an introduction to the spiritual journey: leader's guide.
        p. cm.
Includes bibliographical references.
    ISBN 0-8358-9807-5
    1. Spiritual life—Christianity—Study and teaching. 2. Spiritual formation—Study and teaching. I. Bryant, Stephen D. II. Title.
BV4501.3.T474 2005
248.4'071—dc22

2004029919

Printed in the United States of America

**For more information on *Companions in Christ*
call 1-800-972-0433 or visit www.companionsinchrist.org**

Contents

Weekly Needs at a Glance

Review this Weekly Needs at a Glance list to familiarize yourself with items needed at the *Exploring the Way* Preparatory Meeting and the other weekly meetings. Knowing well in advance the items required for each meeting will help avoid last-minute crises.

Weekly Materials

ALL MEETINGS

- Candle and cloth for worship table (you may want to use the Companions Circle of Friends Candleholder, available online at www.upperroom.org/bookstore/)

- Hymnals, songbooks, or other arrangements for music (tapes/CDs and player)

- Extra Bibles

- "Basic Guidelines for Spiritual Formation Groups and Classes" from the Preparatory Meeting, printed on newsprint and posted in your meeting room

- Newsprint and markers or chalkboard/whiteboard

PREPARATORY MEETING

- Participant's Book for each person

- Several copies of the Companions *Journal* for those who wish to purchase one

- "Basic Guidelines for Spiritual Formation Groups and Classes" written in advance on newsprint (page 22)

- Five parts of every *Exploring the Way* group meeting (Opening, Sharing Insights, Setting the Stage, Taste and See, Closing) written in advance on newsprint (page 22)

- Extra paper and pens for the journaling exercise (journaling pages provided at the back of the Participant's Book)

- Card titled "Prayers for Our *Exploring the Way* Group" from the back of this Leader's Guide

- Notebook paper available for "Practice" portion of the session, if needed

WEEK 1 BEGINNING THE JOURNEY
- Initial "Birth . . . Death" time line (as described under "Setting the Stage," page 29) drawn on newsprint. Further marks will be made on the time line as the session progresses.

WEEK 2 SHARING THE ADVENTURE
- Optional: Pictures of a sailboat, trellised plant, and campfire to illustrate the three metaphors for spiritual discipline on pages 49–50

- Drawings on newsprint of three pictograms as shown on page 47 (Point 4 of "Setting the Stage")

- Two questions for paired sharing in "Taste and See" (page 51) written on newsprint

WEEK 3 BREAD FOR THE JOURNEY
- Selected scripture references for the exercise under "Launching into the Depths" (page 59), written on newsprint

- The diagrams found on page 56 under Point 2 of "Setting the Stage" on newsprint

- The four *R* words of *lectio divina* (page 60) written on newsprint for "Taste and See"

- Questions for debriefing *lectio divina* experience (page 61) written on newsprint

WEEK 4 DRINK FOR THE JOURNEY
- The Lord's Prayer written on newsprint

- A bell or chime for use during the "Taste and See" experience

WEEK 5 COMPANIONS ON THE WAY

- Enough copies of the "Holy Listening" handout that appears at the end of this Leader's Guide session (pages 79–80)

- A bell or chime to ring at halfway point of Holy Listening exercise

WEEK 6 REACHING OUT IN LOVE

- Five underlined portions of review list under Point 1, "Setting the Stage" (pages 84–85)

- Questions for "Closing" (page 89) printed on newsprint

- Optional: Sign-up sheets for next Companions in Christ (or other resource) groups

Acknowledgments

The original twenty-eight week *Companions in Christ* resource grew from the seeds of a vision long held by Stephen D. Bryant, editor and publisher of Upper Room Ministries. It was given shape by Marjorie J. Thompson, director of the Pathways Center for Congregational Spirituality, which houses the Companions in Christ initiative of Upper Room Ministries. The vision, which has now expanded into the Companions in Christ series, was realized through the efforts of many people over many years. The original advisers, consultants, authors, editors, and test churches are acknowledged in the foundational twenty-eight week resource, as well as in the second title of the series, *Companions in Christ: The Way of Forgiveness*. We continue to owe an immense debt of gratitude to each person and congregation there named.

Exploring the Way: An Introduction to the Spiritual Journey is the fifth title in the Companions in Christ series and is intended to be both a bridge resource to the twenty-eight-week resource and a stand-alone resource. The development of *Exploring the Way* is in direct response to the needs expressed by churches and groups around the country for a brief introductory Companions resource that churches can use again and again to orient their members to the spiritual life and to increase participation in spiritual-formation groups in their church.

The progression for the six-week journey through *Exploring the Way* and the writing of the spiritual exercises and compiling of articles found in the Participant's Book are the work of Marjorie Thompson. Marjorie Thompson and Stephen Bryant wrote the material in the Leader's Guide. A staff advisory team comprised of Marjorie Thompson, Stephen Bryant, Cindy Helms, Robin Pippin, and Tony Peterson contributed to the development of this resource. In addition, Companions trainers and others offered valuable insight and guidance for developing *Exploring the Way*. This group included Eileen Campbell-Reed, Schuyler Bissell, Carol Brown, Doris A. Miller, Frank Granger, Carolyn Shapard, Judy Prather, Bo Prosser, Lynn Dyke, Barbara Cavalluzzi, Tim Goss, Jorene Swift, Sarah Bentley, Evie Waack, Drew Henderson, Zora Rockney, David Bowen, Taylor Mills, and Gail Burns.

A group of Companions trainers led test groups in their congregations or ministry settings that have offered valuable insight and guidance for developing *Exploring the Way*. The trainers and congregations represented by the groups include the following: Beth Link McConnell, Providence Baptist Church, Charlotte, NC; Lisa Gray-Lion, Chelsea First United Methodist Church, Chelsea, MI; Mary Jayne Allen, First Baptist Church of Chattanooga, Chattanooga, TN; Devita Parnell, Highland Hills Baptist Church, Macon, GA.

Introduction

Welcome to *Exploring the Way: An Introduction to the Spiritual Journey.* The design of this *Companions in Christ* resource allows small groups and classes to experience a sampling of the spiritual practices that the core *Companions in Christ* resource presents and to lay a foundation for participation in *Companions in Christ* groups. We hope that this resource will serve as a bridge to the twenty-eight-week foundational resource that explores in depth the Christian spiritual life under five headings: Journey, Scripture, Prayer, Call, and Spiritual Guidance.

Exploring the Way has been developed in direct response to the expressed need of churches and groups around the country for a succinct introductory *Companions* resource. Churches can use the resource again and again to orient their members to the spiritual life and to increase participation in the churches' spiritual formation groups. *Exploring the Way* will meet the need for:

- *More information about spiritual formation.* While the number of resources in spirituality burgeon, individuals and congregations need more explanation about commonly used terms and the relation of spiritual practices to scripture and Christian tradition.

- *A basic, introductory* Companions in Christ *resource* to lay a foundation for the longer, in-depth study.

- *A shorter, one-hour format* that fits easily into Sunday night, Wednesday night, or even church school class time frames. This resource, with sessions designed for a full hour, can be fruitfully expanded to one and a half hours.

- *A user-friendly resource* for repeated use to begin leavening the culture of the church and infusing spiritual formation into various aspects of its common life.

- *A resource for longtime church members new to spiritual formation and for those new to the Christian faith.* Time and again, lifelong church attenders experience practices such as *lectio divina* and lament, "Why haven't I known about this way of reading scripture before now?" For those new to the Christian faith, introduction to spiritual formation and spiritual practices can lay a solid and attractive foundation for a lifetime of spiritual growth.

About the Resource and Process

The structure of *Exploring the Way* differs somewhat from other resources in the Companions in Christ series. In the original series, the Participant's Book features individual reading and daily exercises to prepare for the weekly group meeting, while the Leader's Guide provides instructions for a weekly two-hour, small-group meeting.

In *Exploring the Way*, the Participant's Book largely follows the outline of the class or group meeting rather than preparing for it. The Leader's Guide has more information for the leader to convey. Leaders are encouraged to review each session carefully beforehand so they can communicate as much of this information in their own words as possible. As in previous Leader's Guides, concepts or instructions to be spoken directly to the group appear in semibold type. While the sessions are written for a full one-hour format, "Expanded Options" encourage further discusssion and allow the group or class to meet for a preferred ninety minutes.

The Participant's Book contains

- A chapter for each week's topic (see Contents page).

- An outline of points made in the "Setting the Stage" part of the meeting, with space for participants to add their own notes.

- Brief articles to read during the week on the topic of the meeting.

- A page describing the spiritual practice or discipline for the week, based on the "Taste and See" portion of the meeting.

- Specific spiritual exercises for strengthening an awareness of God, related to the weekly spiritual practice and for use the week after its introduction.

- Blank journal pages to record reflections, prayers, and questions related to spiritual exercises during the week and also during class time. Participants will use these notes for later review and reference at the weekly meeting. For those who need more room to write or who prefer a separate, lined journal, we recommend the Companions in Christ *Journal.*

The Participant's Book is a necessary resource during the meeting itself and in the week that follows. Each week includes the outline of "Setting the Stage" for ease of note-taking. The week following the meeting recaps the spiritual practice, and the spiritual exercises offer a setting for personal spiritual formation. Strongly encourage your group members to make use of these exercises each week to gain maximum benefit from the class.

The weekly meeting includes a brief opening worship ("Opening"), time for sharing insights from the past week's reading and exercises ("Sharing Insights"), a time for learning more about the week's spiritual practice ("Setting the Stage"), a time to experience the spiritual practice together ("Taste and See"), and then a short closing worship ("Closing").

The material in *Exploring the Way* covers a period of seven weeks: a preparatory meeting followed by six weeks of content:

1. *Beginning the Journey*—Explores a definition of spiritual formation as a lifelong process of being shaped according to the image of Christ for the sake of the world. Spiritual practice: journaling

2. *Sharing the Adventure*—Explores the adventure of life with God and the role of spiritual disciplines in helping us become more intentional on the path toward God. Spiritual practice: sharing our faith journeys

3. *Bread for the Journey*—Explores scriptural meditation as a powerful means of spiritual formation and nourishment for the journey. Spiritual practice: *lectio divina* (meditating on scripture)

4. *Drink for the Journey*—Explores prayer as a way to pay attention to the divine by "practicing the presence of God" on the daily journey. Spiritual practice: breath prayer, a way to pray without ceasing

5. *Companions on the Way*—Explores the gift of one another, learning how close attention to others helps us pay closer attention to God. Spiritual practice: holy listening

6. *Reaching Out in Love*—Explores a way of noticing God's presence in daily life that leads us beyond ourselves and into God's call to reach out to the world. Spiritual practice: daily examen

The Companions in Christ Network

An added dimension of *Exploring the Way* is the *Companions in Christ* Network. The *Companions* website, www.companionsinchrist.org, includes a discussion room where you can offer insights, voice questions, and respond to others in an ongoing process of shared learning. The site lists *Companions in Christ* groups and their geographical locations so you can make contact as you feel led. Locations and dates for Leader Orientation training events (basic one-day training) and Leader Training events (advanced three-day training) are posted here. This information will help you, especially if you plan to follow *Exploring the Way* with the *Companions in Christ* foundational resource.

The Role of the Leader

In *Exploring the Way*, the leader of the class or group combines the functions of a teacher, who imparts information, along with the role of a group leader who facilitates spiritual growth in the participants. In a class, you generally have specific information (facts, definitions, interpretations, and instructions) that you want to convey. *Exploring the Way* contains some information to grasp, but the intent of each class segment is spiritual formation.

As a leader, you will read the Participant's Book material and complete the spiritual exercises along with group members. This allows you to bring your own responses and questions to the group meeting. Beyond a basic teaching role, you lead by offering your honest reflections and by enabling group members to listen carefully to one another and to the Spirit in their midst.

Leading this kind of formational group requires particular qualities:

Patience and trust. Spiritual formation is a lifelong process. You may not identify any great leaps forward during the six weeks of group study. It may take a while before group members adjust to the purpose and style of a more formational group process.

Listening. This does not mean listening for people to say what you hope they will say so that you can jump in and reinforce them. You will listen for what is actually being said. What is happening in participants' minds and hearts may differ greatly from what you expect after reading the material and doing the exercises yourself.

Accepting. Accept that participants may have had spiritual experiences quite unlike yours and that people often see common experiences in various ways. Your modeling of acceptance will foster acceptance of differences within the group. A primary expression of acceptance comes in permission giving. Permit people to grow and share at their own pace. Let the learners know at the first meeting that while you will encourage full participation in every part of the class process, they may opt out at any point; you will force no one to share or pray without consent. "Where the Spirit of the Lord is, there is freedom" (2 Cor. 3:17).

In the Preparatory Meeting (see pages 19–25) you will establish some basic ground rules for group sharing. Posting these ground rules in a visible place for the first several meetings reminds participants to maintain a safe place for healthy sharing.

A General Outline of Each Group Meeting

The weekly sessions will follow the outline below. Within the outline are three general movements:

1. *Sharing Insights:* Sharing learnings and questions from the prior week's reading and spiritual exercises

2. *Setting the Stage:* Developing an understanding of the week's theme and featured spiritual practice

3. *Taste and See:* Experiencing together a spiritual practice that will lead to individual practice the following week, using the spiritual exercises for guidance

Consider carefully the setting for your class or group meetings. An adaptable space facilitates group process. If you have a small class, one helpful arrangement is a circle of comfortable chairs or sofas. Or participants might want a surface for writing or drawing. Since the class will sometimes break into pairs or clusters, space to separate is crucial. The space for meeting will need to be relatively quiet and peaceful.

A visual symbol can focus the group's attention, especially in opening and closing worship times. A candle on a cloth-covered table in a central place may be all you need to provide this focus. Talk with group members in the Preparatory Meeting about how the worship times help create a formational environment for learning; many may be unfamiliar with this style in a class setting.

OPENING (5 MINUTES)

This brief worship will give participants a chance to quiet down and prepare for the session to follow. The Leader's Guide offers specific suggestions, but you may develop your own pattern of prayer and centering, adapting it to what works best in the group. Possibilities for this opening worship include (1) singing several verses of a hymn together or listening to a selected song on tape or CD, (2) silence, (3) lighting a candle, (4) scripture or other reading (5) individual prayer, or (6) group prayer.

SHARING INSIGHTS (10 MINUTES)

This portion of the meeting allows a little time for individuals to talk about their experience with the spiritual exercises from the past week, the article read, or any life experiences from the past week that relate to last week's theme. Since the content of this time depends on interaction with the Participant's Book during the prior week, stress the importance of engaging in the spiritual exercises each week. Encourage participants to use the journal pages in their Participant's Book during the week and bring it to class to refresh their memories of what they wrote. The sharing will need to be specific and brief. Be prepared to model this with your own succinct response to one of the exercises. If sharing seems sparse, move on to the "Setting the Stage" portion of the meeting.

SETTING THE STAGE (20 MINUTES)

This part of the meeting conveys information, facilitates discussion about the weekly theme, and introduces the spiritual practice learners will experience in the "Taste and See" segment. This content will help group members explore the weekly theme in greater depth.

Be sure to read through the material early in the week so that you have time to think through how to make it your own, as well as to prepare diagrams or other teaching materials on newsprint or PowerPoint (if you prefer this medium).

Review all the Expanded Options within the session outline for possibilities that might work well with your particular group. We highly recommend the ninety-minute time frame as it provides for a richer time of sharing with less pressure.

TASTE AND SEE (20 MINUTES)

This experiential part of the meeting gives time to try out a spiritual practice together. Hopefully such experience will whet the appetite for further spiritual practice. The spiritual exercises in the Participant's Book offer more guided opportunities to "practice the practice" in the week after the meeting. It will require thoughtful preparation to comfortably guide the process in this part of the meeting. Review the material prior to the meeting so you have time to think through each process and complete any preparation.

CLOSING (5 MINUTES)

As it began, the group meeting ends with a brief time of worship. It is a good time to emphasize the importance of doing several spiritual exercises in the Participant's Book during the week ahead. The Leader's Guide includes specific suggestions for the "Closing," but you may want to customize them to meet the needs of your group.

Concluding Matters

Consider ahead of time the song or hymn selections for the "Opening" and "Closing" each week. In the hymnals or songbooks available to you, look for singable tunes with thematically appropriate words. If your group sings reluctantly, get several audiocassette tapes or CDs to play and invite "sing-alongs."

In addition to traditional hymns and contemporary praise songs, a new repertoire of contemplative song and chant is emerging from communities such as Taizé and Iona. Some of these pieces can be found in *The Faith We Sing* (TFWS), an ecumenical and international songbook published by Abingdon Press as a supplement to *The United Methodist Hymnal*. (See order information in the Annotated Resource List on pages 96–104 of this Leader's Guide.) Iona Community songs, also ecumenical and international in scope, can be found or ordered through many religious bookstores.

When the Leader's Guide suggests songs for certain meetings, please note they are suggestions only. Each group will have access to different hymnals and songbooks and may have its own preference in musical style.

The purpose of the Companions in Christ series is to equip persons of faith with both personal and corporate spiritual life practices that will continue long beyond the time frame of this particular resource. Participants may continue certain disciplines on their own and carry some practices into congregational life. Others may desire the continuation of a small group, in which case we urge serious consideration of the *Companions in Christ* foundational twenty-eight-week resource.

As you guide your group through this six-week journey, you will discover that certain topics generate interest and energy for further exploration. Some participants may wish that certain readings or weekly meetings could go into more depth. When the group expresses strong desire to continue with a particular topic or practice, take special note of it. A number of possibilities exists for small-group study and practice beyond this resource. Some suggested resources are in the Annotated Resource List on pages 96–104. The group will need to decide future directions toward the end of this experience.

Our prayer for you as a leader is that the weeks ahead will lead you and your group to explore the way of life that leads to your transformation according to the image of Christ, for the sake of the world. May your companionship with Christ and with one another be richly blessed!

Preparatory Meeting

PREPARATION

Pray for the class and each person in it. Pray for a listening spirit and fresh insight as you prepare to teach. Pray also for a hospitable heart and centeredness in God's presence as you lead the class.

Review the entire class process. Select a scripture text for the "Opening," appropriate songs for both "Opening" and "Closing" (optional), and a benediction for the "Closing." Prepare newsprint or PowerPoint materials as needed (see especially five parts of class process and ground rules). Have paper and pens available for the "Practice" portion of today's meeting.

Read the notes below carefully, underlining sections you wish to emphasize. Put the basic ideas into your own words and expand on any portions with your own experience, stories, or illustrations.

Prepare the space before class begins. Near the center of the teaching space, set a small table with a cloth and candle as a focal point for worship and reflection. Arrange for newsprint or PowerPoint equipment as needed.

OPENING (10 MINUTES)

Welcome the class, creating a warm and relaxed tone.

Set a context for the six-week experience to come.

- **Our meeting today will prepare us to participate in a new venture called** *Exploring the Way.*

- This experiential class in spiritual formation guides us through a six-week journey with God and with one another.

- Our aim is to discover what the Christian spiritual life is about and which spiritual practices can help us live more freely and faithfully as followers of Jesus.

Join together in worship.

- Since we're exploring the spiritual life, we will begin each meeting with worship to remind us that we gather in God's presence, seeking divine guidance. I will light this candle each time we meet as a sign of Christ's light among us. (light candle)

- *Read a short scripture passage.* Suggestion: Psalm 63:1 (read unhurriedly and with meaning):

> O God, you are my God, I seek you,
>> my soul thirsts for you;
> my flesh faints for you,
>> as in a dry and weary land where there is no water.

- *Offer a brief prayer* of your own or use this one:

> Gracious God,
> As we journey through *Exploring the Way*, open our hearts to seek you that we might be aware of your guiding presence with us step by step. In Jesus' name. Amen.

INTRODUCE THE RESOURCE AND OURSELVES (15 MINUTES)

Indicate the twofold intent of this Preparatory Meeting:

1. to introduce the six-week experience
2. to introduce ourselves to one another

Introduce the basic purpose and goal of class (group)

- This is our preparation for six classes that introduce the basics of the Christian spiritual life. *Exploring the Way* is for those of us who consider ourselves beginners in the spiritual life, whether we've been in the church a long time or are new to the faith. In a sense, we are all beginners. Thomas Merton, one of the spiritual giants of the twentieth century, said, "We do not want to be beginners. But let us be convinced of the fact that we will never be anything else but beginners, all our life!"[1]

- As beginners, we will learn some basic language of spirituality and spiritual formation, terms you have probably heard but may want to understand better and have a chance to discuss.

- This class will cover some general information about Christian spirituality and its disciplines; but more importantly, it will give you a chance to try out key practices, ways of being more aware of and open to God. You will have a chance to "taste and see" these spiritual practices for yourselves. As the psalmist says, "O taste and see that the LORD is good" (Psalm 34:8).

- The goal is to discover how certain practices can help us know the reality of God and live a deeper, more Spirit-directed life. We want to find one or two practices that feel like a good fit to make a part of our lives as maturing Christians.

Introduce ourselves. (Adjust time as needed for larger class.)

- Invite participants to introduce themselves briefly by saying their name and a few words about what drew them to this group. Encourage honest speech and attentive listening.

- As leader, model self-introduction by going first and keeping it short. Invite others to follow you.

OVERVIEW OF EXPLORING THE WAY (15 MINUTES)

Let's take a closer look now at the Participant's Book, our class process, and some basic guidelines for being together. (Pass out Participant's Books.)

Review the Participant's Book and weekly expectations.

Have everyone open their books as you go over these points. Use Week 1 to illustrate weekly material.

- A chapter for each week (see Contents page)
- An outline of points made in the meeting with space to add your own notes
- A brief article to read during the week on the subject of the meeting
- A page describing the spiritual discipline or practice for the week
- Specific spiritual exercises that encourage the practice of that discipline to develop an awareness of God during the week

- Quotes for Further Reflection
- A glossary of definitions and FAQs (frequently asked questions) at the back of the Participant's Book
- Journal pages at the back of the Participant's Book

Explain the Class/Group Process (refer to the five parts listed on newsprint or PowerPoint)

- *Opening*: Each week begins with worship to center us in God's presence
- *Sharing Insights*: Brief time to share discoveries, questions, or insights from reading and spiritual practice during the week
- *Setting the Stage*: Presentation of basic information combined with short exercises or discussion to help assimilate the information content
- *Taste and See*: Experiential learning time for "taste-testing" a particular spiritual practice
- *Closing*: Class reminders and worship to conclude time together

Clarify the time frame chosen for this class/group meeting.

- Be sure participants understand the expectations for the time commitment of each meeting.
- If you need to discuss and agree upon a longer time frame, build into this Preparatory Meeting time for such a decision.
- Remember, you are free to offer this as a one-hour class or to add content/process enrichment to build a ninety-minute meeting time.

Basic Guidelines for Spiritual Formation Groups and Classes

- **Basic ground rules that create safe space, a listening environment, and freedom to grow govern healthy interactions in the spiritual life. Some examples:** (list on newsprint or PowerPoint)
  1. **Speak only for yourself about your feelings, beliefs, and experience.**
  2. **Maintain confidentiality. What members share in the group stays in the group.**
  3. **Respect and receive what others offer, even if you disagree.**
  4. **Honor the way God works in different individuals.**
  5. **Share only what and when you choose.**

- We will make every effort to follow these guidelines during our six weeks together and gently remind one another of them if necessary.

- Spiritual formation is not debate over biblical interpretation or theological issues. It focuses on learning and sharing the benefits of spiritual practice in daily life.

- Spiritual formation is not therapy or advice giving. We come together to direct our thoughts toward God's presence, help, and guidance; not to fix one another's personal problems.

Encourage class members to use the Participant's Book to maximum advantage, especially the opportunity to try out basic spiritual practices. Establish the expectation that each person will commit to trying at least two or three of the daily exercises each week. Remind them that their book use will help them benefit from the class. The book includes journaling pages. *Invite responses/questions/clarifications* before moving on.

> Ask: **How does this approach strike you? Does this sound like a process of learning and growing that you want to participate in?**

(Allow any and all responses. If negative responses arise, encourage participants to try it one week at a time, giving themselves the opportunity to experience it before deciding not to attend.)

EXPLORING SPIRITUAL-FORMATION LANGUAGE AND PRACTICE (10 MINUTES)

Let's think a bit about the spiritual-life language we often hear these days: terms like *spirituality, spiritual formation,* **and** *spiritual disciplines.* **What do you think the word** *spirituality* **means? What connotations does it carry for you?** *(invite responses)*

Direct the class members to page 10 of their Participant's Book. Ask a volunteer to read aloud the quote by Elizabeth O'Connor, one of the founders of The Church of the Savior in Washington, DC:

> That is what Christianity is all about—becoming lovers. The mission of the Church is just loving people. And our confession? What is our confession? It is that we do not know how to love. Until we have made that confession, there is nothing to be learned. We cannot even be a beginner with the beginners, and in the School of Christianity there is nothing else to be but a beginner.[2]

- Invite reflection on and response to the quote: **What ideas or phrases stand out? How do they shed light on our thinking about spirituality or the Christian spiritual life?**

- Talk briefly about spiritual disciplines as *practices* that help us learn to live by love and so can lead to our transformation in Christ. Invite the group members to identify spiritual disciplines with which they are familiar (in theory or practice), and list these on newsprint.

- As leader, share a few of the spiritual practices that have been most important to you in your faith journey; then ask others to say aloud what they have tried. What worked or didn't work? What feelings and images do people carry with them concerning spiritual disciplines?

Mention the spiritual disciplines or practices the class will consider over the course of these six weeks.

Direct the learners to "Six Spiritual Practices for the Journey" (page 18, Participant's Book):

1. *Journaling*—tracking your faith experiences and responses in writing.

2. *Sharing spiritual journeys*—learning to share facets of your faith journey with others for insight, support, and encouragement

3. *Lectio divina*—the classic practice of spiritual reading or "praying the scriptures"

4. *Breath prayer*—a simple way to pray through the day with a short phrase

5. *Holy listening*—the practice of deep and attentive listening to one another

6. *Daily examen*—looking back over a twenty-four-hour period with an eye to God's presence and your response in the day

PRACTICE (5 MINUTES)

(Refer participants to the journal pages in the back of their Participant's Book. Also have paper available for those who would prefer that.)

Now let's try a quick exercise. Take a few minutes to respond to this question: "When in your life were you particularly aware of God's presence or guidance?" You may use words, symbols, images, or phrases to record your response on paper.

After three to four minutes, point out that reflecting on our lives by jotting down thoughts in words, symbols, images, or phrases is the beginning of journaling (first spiritual practice on the list).

- To journal means to keep a record of thoughts, feelings, questions, and insights over time.
- Journaling is one spiritual practice that helps us pay attention to God's presence in daily life. It can help us notice God's guidance and respond to it.
- The Participant's Book for Week 1 provides more information on journaling, as well as suggested exercises to help you explore this spiritual practice. Feel free to look ahead at those exercises and start practicing this week if you wish.

CLOSING (5 MINUTES)

Sing a hymn or song verse (optional).

Invite a time of quiet reflection. **What are your hopes for the time ahead of us as companions in Christ? What are your anxieties about these next weeks together? Present both your hopes and your fears to God in silent prayer now.**

Offer a brief word of prayer, asking that all might be able to release their hopes and concerns into God's gracious hands. End with thanksgiving for each person and for God's good purposes in bringing this group together.

Encourage participants to try at least one or two of the exercises for Week 1. They will also have time the week after the next meeting to practice journaling.

Offer a closing benediction.

Week 1
Beginning the Journey

PREPARATION

Pray for the class and each person in it. Pray for a listening spirit and fresh insight as you prepare to teach. Pray also for a hospitable heart and centeredness in God's presence as you lead the class.

Review the entire class process. Select an appropriate song or hymn for the "Opening" and a scripture text for the "Closing." Prepare newsprint or PowerPoint materials as needed.

Read this session guide carefully, underlining sections you wish to emphasize. Put the basic ideas into your own words and expand on any portions you wish to with Expanded Options or with your own experience, stories, or illustrations.

Expanded Class Options: To build a ninety-minute session, draw from the materials that are set off in boxes. Use your discretion to shape class time.

Prepare the space before class begins. Near the center of the teaching space, set a small table with a cloth and candle as a focal point for worship and reflection. Arrange for newsprint/PowerPoint equipment as needed.

OPENING (5 MINUTES)

Welcome the class, creating a warm and relaxed tone.

Set a context for this week's theme and spiritual practice.

This is the first of six classes that explore the basics of the Christian spiritual life. We want to begin seeing our lives as a sacred journey and to understand that the journey's aim is to become more like Christ. To be formed in the likeness of Jesus Christ is the meaning of *spiritual formation*.

Join together in worship.

- Let's open our time together by lighting this candle to remind us of God's presence with us here and now.

- *Read Psalm 139:1-2:*

  O LORD, you have searched me and known me.
  You know when I sit down and when I rise up;
  > you discern my thoughts from far away.

- *Sing a song of your own choosing (optional).*

- *Offer a brief spontaneous prayer or use this suggested prayer:*

  O Lord, our God, grant us grace to desire you with our whole heart,
  that desiring, we may seek and find you; and finding you, we may
  love you; and loving you we may fulfill the purpose for which you
  have made us. Amen. (Adapted from Saint Anselm, 1033–1109)

SHARING INSIGHTS (10 MINUTES)

Today we will explore the idea of our lives as a sacred journey. The spiritual discipline
we will consider in relation to our life journeys is attentiveness to God's presence.
And one of the most effective ways to be attentive is to look reflectively at our lives
through the practice of journaling.

In last week's Preparatory Meeting we tried an easy journaling exercise, and I encouraged you to look at the week ahead to try out one or two of the weekly exercises. Did
you try out any journaling this week? If so, how did it help you become more aware
of God's presence?

Allow responses to surface. If no one tried any exercises, simply indicate that we will talk
more about journaling toward the end of today's meeting. Encourage participants to think
about journaling as an easy endeavor rather than a complicated or burdensome task.

SETTING THE STAGE (15 MINUTES)

Introducing the Spiritual Journey

LEADER NOTE

I once set out from a dark point, the Womb, and now I proceed to another dark point, the Tomb. . . . We come from a dark abyss, we end in a dark abyss, and we call the luminous interval life.

I have one longing only: to grasp what is hidden behind appearances, to ferret out that mystery which brings me to birth and then kills me, to discover if behind the visible and unceasing stream of the world an invisible and immutable presence is hiding.[1]

—Nikos Kazantzakis

Draw the following diagram on newsprint or board, and direct the class to page 11 in the Participant's Book under "Setting the Stage." You will add to the diagram at various points, ending up with the full diagram as seen on the bottom of page 31 of this Leader's Guide.

Birth . . . . Life as we know it . . . . Death

Introduce two views of life and explore the meaning of spiritual formation:

1. *One view: Life is a journey from "womb to tomb."*

   The writer Nikos Kazantzakis refers to life as the "luminous interval" between the womb and the tomb. We are familiar with the portion of life that begins at birth and ends with death. Between these bookends lie many milestones: birthdays, graduations, marriage, career achievements, retirement, and so on.

2. *Another view: Life is a sacred journey encompassed by the mystery of God.*

Biblical faith provides a more expansive view. It sees the journey of life extending beyond what we are familiar with and entirely encompassed by the gracious mystery of God. (Draw a large oval around the time line and write "The Mystery of God" below the diagram.)

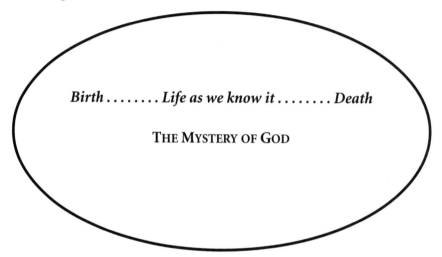

Birth . . . . *Life as we know it* . . . . Death

THE MYSTERY OF GOD

(Draw arrows pointing left and right above "Birth" and "Death" on the time line. Write "Farther Out" between the two arrows. See diagram on top of page 31.)

- **In the second view, the sacred journey of life extends both "farther out" and "further in."**

- **It extends "farther out" in both directions, since we know by faith that we begin in God and end in God. As Ignatius of Loyola once said, "I come from God, I belong to God, I return to God."[2]**

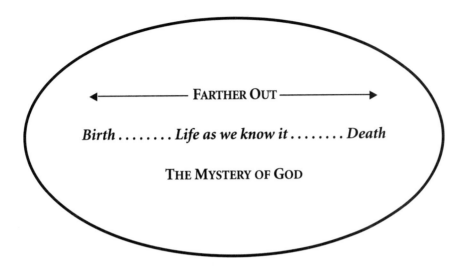

- **It also extends "further in"—below the surface of daily life to the deep, holy gift of life here and now, the depth that allows us to discover the mystery of God.** (Draw an arrow pointing down from "Life as we know it"; write "Further In" vertically; your diagram will now look like this:)

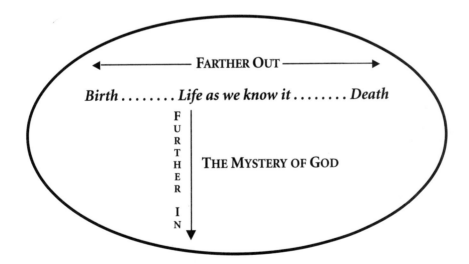

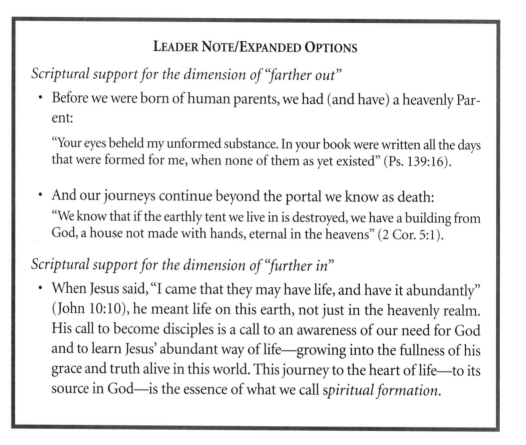

LEADER NOTE/EXPANDED OPTIONS

Scriptural support for the dimension of "farther out"

- Before we were born of human parents, we had (and have) a heavenly Parent:

  "Your eyes beheld my unformed substance. In your book were written all the days that were formed for me, when none of them as yet existed" (Ps. 139:16).

- And our journeys continue beyond the portal we know as death:

  "We know that if the earthly tent we live in is destroyed, we have a building from God, a house not made with hands, eternal in the heavens" (2 Cor. 5:1).

Scriptural support for the dimension of "further in"

- When Jesus said, "I came that they may have life, and have it abundantly" (John 10:10), he meant life on this earth, not just in the heavenly realm. His call to become disciples is a call to an awareness of our need for God and to learn Jesus' abundant way of life—growing into the fullness of his grace and truth alive in this world. This journey to the heart of life—to its source in God—is the essence of what we call *spiritual formation.*

Consider the meaning of spiritual formation.

So this sacred journey of our lives extends from before our birth until long after our death, encompassed in God's mystery. Christian faith tells us the purpose of the "luminous interval" between birth and death is to be shaped according to Christ's image. This is the basic idea behind the phrase *spiritual formation.* Let's explore this idea further.

- Ask the class members what the term *spiritual formation* means to them. When they hear the expression, what comes to mind? Let them jot down ideas in their journaling pages, then receive a few responses aloud.

- Invite them to ponder this definition: "Spiritual formation is the process of being shaped according to the image of Christ by the gracious working of the Holy Spirit, for the sake of the world." Suggest that they look at this definition in the Participant's Book on page 14.

- Discuss points of response, interest, clarification, and struggle.

- Ask several people to read aloud the scripture passages below that speak to our spiritual formation (page 13, Participant's Book). Say a few words about the texts as indicated.

SCRIPTURAL FOUNDATIONS FOR SPIRITUAL FORMATION

Beloved, we are God's children now; what we will be has not yet been revealed. What we do know is this:...we will be like him [Christ] (1 John 3:2). We are called to journey by the grace of God into the full potential of who we are created to be as images of God, reflecting God's love.

Be perfect [mature, complete], therefore, as your heavenly Father is perfect (Matt. 5:48). After teaching that we should love not only those who love us but our enemies as well, Jesus concluded with these words. The Greek term (*teleios*) translated "perfect" here means completion, fullness, maturity in love.

"You shall love the Lord your God with all your heart, and with all your soul, and with all your strength, and with all your mind; and your neighbor as yourself" (Luke 10:25-27). When asked how to inherit eternal life, this was Jesus' reply. It describes how Jesus himself lived—all that he taught and embodied.

I am again in the pain of childbirth until Christ is formed in you (Gal. 4:19). The apostle Paul is clear that Jesus Christ himself is the goal and shape of our life with God.

All of us . . . are being transformed into the same image [the image of Christ] from one degree of glory to another (2 Cor. 3:18).

It is he [Christ[whom we proclaim . . . so that we may present everyone mature in Christ. For this I toil and struggle with all the energy that he powerfully inspires within me (Col. 1:28-29).

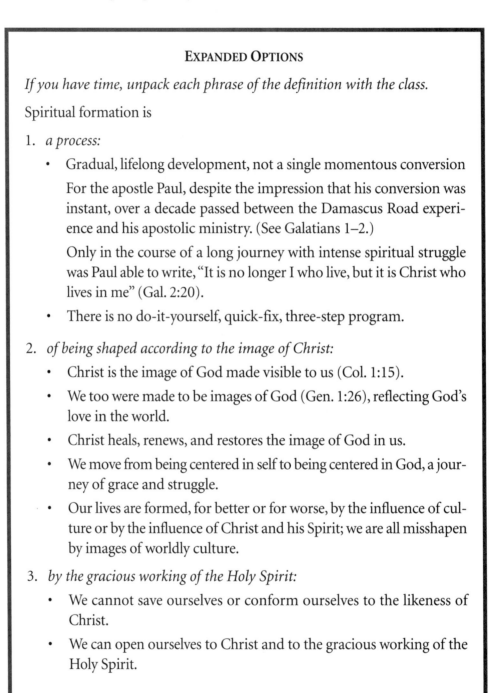

EXPANDED OPTIONS

If you have time, unpack each phrase of the definition with the class.

Spiritual formation is

1. *a process:*

   • Gradual, lifelong development, not a single momentous conversion

     For the apostle Paul, despite the impression that his conversion was instant, over a decade passed between the Damascus Road experience and his apostolic ministry. (See Galatians 1–2.)

     Only in the course of a long journey with intense spiritual struggle was Paul able to write, "It is no longer I who live, but it is Christ who lives in me" (Gal. 2:20).

   • There is no do-it-yourself, quick-fix, three-step program.

2. *of being shaped according to the image of Christ:*

   • Christ is the image of God made visible to us (Col. 1:15).

   • We too were made to be images of God (Gen. 1:26), reflecting God's love in the world.

   • Christ heals, renews, and restores the image of God in us.

   • We move from being centered in self to being centered in God, a journey of grace and struggle.

   • Our lives are formed, for better or for worse, by the influence of culture or by the influence of Christ and his Spirit; we are all misshapen by images of worldly culture.

3. *by the gracious working of the Holy Spirit:*

   • We cannot save ourselves or conform ourselves to the likeness of Christ.

   • We can open ourselves to Christ and to the gracious working of the Holy Spirit.

- The Spirit enables us to choose the way of Christ over the way of self.
- Spiritual disciplines or practices are ways of opening ourselves to the wind of the Spirit.

4. *for the sake of the world:*
   - Our spiritual formation is not just for our own benefit, but for the good of all whom God can touch through us. We are to be salt and light in a world full of blandness and darkness.
   - The spiritual life is not simply about "me" but about our availability to God's love for the world.
   - Our salvation and sanctification (formation in Christ) bear spiritual fruit for which the world desperately hungers: compassion, patience, truthfulness, reconciliation.
   - Transformed persons are the leaven by which God transforms the world.

Summarize the discussion. Draw on the following points in your own words:

- The call to be on a journey of transformation sounds throughout the New Testament. The language of spiritual formation comes directly from Paul's way of speaking. The idea of Christ being formed in us is Paul's way of summarizing the promise of the Christian life. "In him [Christ] the whole fullness of deity dwells bodily"(Col. 2:9). In Christ all divine love and grace becomes visible. Paul's passion in ministry was to "present everyone mature *in Christ*" (emphasis added).

- The New Testament clearly states that the goal of the spiritual journey is our formation in the likeness of Jesus Christ, whose love is offered for the salvation and transformation of the world. We call the process of Christ being formed in us and our maturing in Christ, "spiritual formation."

- The heart of this process is not what we do to form ourselves—trying to be good or moral or to make ourselves more like Jesus. The heart of formation in Christ lies in our openness every day to God's presence and power. God forms us in Christ as we wake up to the invitations of divine love in the midst of our blindness and brokenness.

TASTE AND SEE (20 MINUTES)

Introduce a journaling reflection exercise: "Above and Below the Line"

- Instruct the class members to turn to one of the journaling pages in the Participant's Book and to draw a horizontal line about a third of the way down the page.

- Go back to the diagram drawn earlier, reminding the class of the arrow pointing down to indicate the "further in" dimension of our lives.

- Explain that we will participate in an exercise called "Above and Below the Line." **Above the line we will write words or draw symbols that indicate the external events and milestones that have marked our lives. Below the line we will place words or symbols representing what stirs beneath the surface of appearances— the presence or guidance of God's Spirit that gives depth and meaning to our lives. We aim to identify the "further in" dimension for ourselves.**

- Offer some biblical examples:

  Above the line, the Hebrew people were slaves who escaped from Pharaoh, migrated north, and developed into a little country of their own.

  Below the line, the Hebrew people were a chosen people, subjects of God's liberating action, and a means of God's revelation to all nations.

  Above the line, Jesus was Jesus of Nazareth, son of Joseph and Mary.

  Below the line, Jesus heard God say he was "My Son, the Beloved, with whom I am well pleased" (Matt. 3:17).

EXPANDED OPTIONS

Ask someone to read aloud "Wild West Redemption" (page 15, Participant's Book). Instruct participants, as they listen to the story, to reflect on what is "above the line" for Phyllis and what is happening "below the line." Have them write on a separate time line the words that come to mind. Then invite them to share their reflections.

Guide the exercise as follows:

- **Take some time to reflect on your life. Then above your line, place words or symbols representing three or four milestone events that have deeply affected who you are.** (Allow a few minutes of silence.)

- **Now take time to ponder: Where in the course of your journey have you been marked, blessed, or shaped with an intensified awareness of God in your life or your life in God? . . . Just sit quietly for a while, open to God's presence; let your memory be guided. . . .** (Allow several minutes of silence.)

- **When you are ready, place words or symbols below the line to indicate where your life has been marked by an awareness of God—perhaps a sense of belonging to God or being called by Christ or feeling directed by the Spirit. . . .** (Allow several minutes of silence.)

- **Finally, what scripture verse, biblical image, or hymn comes to mind in association with your life-line diagram? Don't try to think up an answer. Again, sit quietly and allow the Spirit to lead you to a verse, song, or image that fits your life. Write down what comes to mind below the diagram.** (Allow another minute of silence.)

- **Now step back and look at your page. What do you see? What connections do you notice between what is above the line and what is below the line?** (Allow another minute of silence.)

Invite observations. Be prepared to build on participants' observations with thoughts like these:

- What I see are human journeys that extend outward, marked by various events and that also extend inward beneath the surface of events to the depths of their meaning and purpose in shaping our lives.

- I see a fuller, more complete picture of who I am. Above the line I am (name) from (city or state), and I do (title or role). Below the line, I am a child of God, trying to stay alert daily to the grace of God.

Ask: **Where were you aware of God's presence in the course of this exercise?** *Invite responses.*

Closing (10 minutes)

Sing a song: "Surely the Presence of the Lord Is in This Place" (optional)

Read a brief scripture text. (Suggestion: 2 Cor. 3:18)

Invite participants into the week ahead.

I encourage you to use your Participant's Book during the coming week to review key points of our class time and to find more stories and illustrations related to this week's theme. The more you use your Participant's Book, the more you will gain from this course. Remember, the spiritual practice for this week is journaling.

Reinforce the nature and importance of journaling as a spiritual practice.

- **The beginning of journaling comes in reflecting on our lives and jotting down thoughts or questions using words, images, and phrases.**

- **Journaling is a spiritual practice that helps us pay attention to God's presence in daily life. It helps us notice God's guidance and respond to it.**

- **Journaling is the first type of weekly exercise we will practice in *Exploring the Way*. The Participant's Book for this week offers useful illustrations about journaling and several exercises to help us explore this spiritual practice. Let's test them out.**

Say a benediction.

This prayer for the Christians of Ephesus, attributed to Paul, helps us glimpse a vision of the spiritual potential in the sons and daughters of God. Listen as I read this benediction from Ephesians 3:16-19:

> I pray that, according to the riches of his glory, [God] may grant that you may be strengthened in your inner being with power through his Spirit, and that Christ may dwell in your hearts through faith, as you are being rooted and grounded in love. I pray that you may have the power to comprehend, with all the saints, what is the breadth and length and height and depth, and to know the love of Christ that surpasses knowledge, so that you may be filled with all the fullness of God. Amen.

Week 2
Sharing the Adventure

PREPARATION

Pray for the class and each person in it. Pray for a listening spirit and fresh insight as you prepare to teach. Pray also for a hospitable heart and centeredness in God's presence as you lead the class.

Review the entire class process. Select scripture texts and songs for the "Opening" and "Closing" and a benediction for the "Closing." Some suggestions are provided. Prepare newsprint or PowerPoint materials as needed.

Read through "Setting the Stage" carefully, underlining sections you wish to emphasize. Be ready to put the basic ideas into your own words and to expand or adapt material based on your own experience and illustrations. Option: You might consider bringing pictures of a sailboat, trellised plant, and campfire to illustrate the three metaphors for spiritual discipline on pages 49–50 of this Leader's Guide.

Expand the class options: To build a ninety-minute session, draw from the materials that appear in boxes. Use your discretion to shape class time.

Prepare the space before class begins. Near the center of the teaching space, set a small table with a cloth and candle as a focal point for worship and reflection. Feel free to add other symbols that seem appropriate to class content.

OPENING (10 MINUTES)

Welcome the class, creating a warm and relaxed tone.

Set a context for this week's theme and spiritual practice.

> **This week we will explore our spiritual journeys as an adventure into greater intimacy with God. We will discuss our anxieties about getting closer to God and look**

at the role of spiritual disciplines in our growth. Then we'll try out the practice of paying closer attention to God by sharing a little of our faith journeys with one another.

Join together in worship.

- *Light the candle, saying,* **We begin our time together by lighting this candle and becoming aware of God's presence with us here and now.**

- *Read Jeremiah 6:16*

> Thus says the LORD:
> Stand at the crossroads, and look,
> > and ask for the ancient paths,
> where the good way lies; and walk in it,
> > and find rest for your souls.

- *Sing a song such as "Surely the Presence of the Lord Is in This Place"* (optional).

- *Offer a brief prayer.*

SHARING INSIGHTS (10 MINUTES)

Allow participants to share insights or questions arising from last week's meeting, their week's practice of journaling, and/or their reading in the Participant's Book.

SETTING THE STAGE (15 MINUTES)

1. *Review: Life is a sacred journey, the purpose of which is our spiritual formation.*

   Last week we talked about life as a sacred journey, the purpose of which is our increasing likeness to Christ. We explored spiritual formation through a definition: "Spiritual formation is the process of being shaped according to the image of Christ by the gracious working of the Holy Spirit, for the sake of the world."

2. *Our sacred journeys are a lifelong adventure.*

   This week we will continue to explore the sacred journey of life—the amazing adventure of it, the hesitations we have, and the role of spiritual disciplines in supporting and strengthening us for the road ahead. We are talking about being more than wanderers on the journey of life; we are venturing forward, listening for God's call.

- Ask participants to think about the difference between just wandering around and setting out on an adventure. Gather responses. Bring out points like these if they don't surface from the group:

WANDERING	ADVENTURING
· takes no particular preparation	· requires forethought and planning
· fun/serendipitous or confusing/ anxious	· may be delightful or tense
· without clear direction, meandering	· sets out with purpose and direction

Make the point that the Christian spiritual life is an adventure. It has a clear aim, and we can follow intentional paths toward our goal.

LEADER NOTES/EXPANDED OPTIONS

The Bible is filled with stories of people who said yes to God's call and learned to venture forward into life with God as guide. In each case, God called them to a closer relationship, to become part of what God was doing in history, and to share in the divine purpose for humanity. What greater adventure can there be! Examples:

- *Abram and Sarai* became more than nomads when they said yes to the call of God: "Go from your country . . . to the land that I will show you" (Gen. 12:1). Abraham trusted God, becoming God's friend (James 2:23) and an instrument of the birthing of a new nation.

- *Mary* became more than a young girl searching for a decent family life when she heard and responded to God's call. In trust, Mary made herself available to the Holy Spirit and became a participant in God's saving action. Hers was truly a God-bearing life (Luke 1:38).

> • *Peter and John* became more than poor fishermen when they allowed Jesus into their boat (Luke 5:1-11). Hearing Jesus' call, they exchanged an existence of fishing to survive for a transforming journey of fishing with Jesus to heal and redeem people.
>
> You might wish to tell a brief vignette from your own story: when have you moved from wandering through life to discovering the intentional adventure of life with God? How has God become real for you, an intimate and guiding presence along life's way?

• Ask participants to respond inwardly to these questions printed in their Participant's Book, page 21:

(1) When have I undergone a positive change in my relationship with God or felt a new sense of adventure in my faith life?

(2) What spiritual practices or gifts have helped me in this shift?

Invite them to jot down thoughts and leave a few minutes for silence. Mention that you will return to these questions in the "Taste and See" portion of the session.

3. *God calls each of us to a closer relationship.*

The divine call is not simply to do something great but to live close to God, to share God's loving intentions for the world.

• **This relationship matures us, completes our character, and makes us whole; we become who God has created us to be. Our relationship with God is truly the adventure of a lifetime.**

• **Yet we often hesitate to embark on this adventure; we fear responding to God's call. Here is a glimpse into one woman's fear of responding to "the Voice."** (Have someone read aloud "Listening for the Voice" (page 25, Participant's Book.)

• Ask if participants can identify with this woman's fears. Discuss the risk-taking of any true adventure.

- Invite participants to share negative or frightening images of God that can interfere with the desire to draw closer. Then ask what helpful or healing images of God they have discovered for encouragement.

- Point out that our concepts and images of God naturally change over time as we mature. This change is healthy. Offer a few biblical illustrations:

  – Job's understanding of God changes over the course of his many trials.

  – Jesus tells religious leaders they will eventually see how wrong they have been in their notions of God. He stretches people beyond conventional ideas by saying, "You have heard that it was said, . . . But I say to you . . ." (Matt. 5:43-44).

  – Jesus says, "He is God not of the dead, but of the living; you are quite wrong" (Mark 12:27).

- Ask: **When has your image of God changed or matured?** *(Allow for responses.)*

LEADER NOTES/EXPANDED OPTIONS

To expand the class to ninety minutes, build on this segment.

Explore the impact of our images of God:

Being open to a growing intimacy with God may depend on our image of God. The images we hold shape how we choose to relate to this mysterious power. Why would we want to get close to the Almighty if we fear what God might require of us? We hear, "The good die young"; and we say, "God, please notice that I'm not very good!"

Explore in more depth the negative or positive images we may hold.

NEGATIVE IMAGES OF GOD

The terrifying God:

- Angry Judge, wreaking vengeance and throwing lightning bolts at sinners
- Big Policeman, watching for bad behavior and ready to give speeders a ticket
- Capricious Emperor, playing favorites using impenetrable rules

---

The power-play God:

- Authoritarian Parent, demanding obedience out of sheer authority
- The "Princess" who must be adored, worshiped, and attended to—or else
- Retired Executive of the Universe, disinterested and uninvolved in daily life but still expecting dues

The doleful God:

- Heavy Taskmaster, with a "will" that feels like a ten-ton elephant
- Joyless Duty, who expects everyone to sacrifice all and give up every pleasure

The magic God:

- Great Sugar Daddy, dispensing wishes upon request (variant of Big Santa)
- Cosmic Bellhop, helping out in background when people can't get it done their way

Invite class discussion:

- *Let the members respond to the unhelpful images*, naming some they have grown up with and adding further images if they wish.
- *Invite them to name some helpful images of God* they have grown up with or discovered. List these on newsprint/board.
- If not named, you might include the following: The Good Shepherd, Lover of Souls, Great Protector (eagle with young and "He watching over Israel" or other biblical images), Ocean of Love (hymn reference from "Joyful, Joyful"), Light of lights, Prince of Peace, Suffering Servant, and so forth.

4. *Consider three pictures of how we relate to God*

Our comfort level in getting close to God is influenced not only by our image of God but by our notion of how we are related. Let's look at some pictures of how we view this relationship. (Point to three images on newsprint and in Participant's Book, page 23.)

God is "above us," out there; our job is to connect	*God is within us, in our heart/ soul*	*We live within God's being, can't exist apart from God*

"O that you would tear open the heavens and come down" (Isa. 64:1).

On the day I called, you answered me" (Ps. 138:3).

"The word is very near to you; . . . in your mouth and in your heart" (Deut. 30:14).

Your body is a temple of the Holy Spirit" (1 Cor. 6:19).

"Christ in you, the hope of glory" (Col. 1:27).

"In him we live and move and have our being" (Acts 17:28).

"Abide in me as I abide in you" (John 15:4).

"Your life is hidden with Christ in God" (Col. 3:3).

- *Point out the three pictograms.* Explain that they represent three ways of understanding our relationship to God. Each image has roots in scripture and contains its own truth; we may move among these images as we think about/relate to God.

- *Invite participants to identify the pictogram that best represents how they view their relationship with God.* Ask if one picture seems more complete than the others.

- *Note briefly the implications of each image for spiritual formation.* The first image keeps us in a more "informational" mode of relationship with God. As we perceive distance between us, we tend to want/need information about God and try to find ways to make ourselves known/heard by God. The other two images tend to open us to a more "formational" way of learning. We perceive that God desires to be known and loved at the core of our being and that we cannot know ourselves apart from God's life.

5. *Examine the role of spiritual disciplines.*

- Invite a brief discussion of the meaning of spiritual discipline:

    - **Embracing some form of spiritual discipline indicates our intention to move forward on the adventure of coming close to God.**

    - Open a discussion of participants' understanding of spiritual discipline: how they feel about the word *discipline* and which disciplines are familiar to them.

- Offer some theological perspectives to increase their understanding:

    - **Spiritual disciplines are practices that help us refocus our lives on God, so that the Spirit can reshape our attitudes and actions in Christ's likeness. They are a means for our spiritual formation.**

    - **Spiritual disciplines are not ways to prove our righteousness. They are a way of fostering trust in and receptivity to God. They make room for grace to operate in our lives.**

- Read Philippians 2:12-13. Point out how these verses help us see the relationship between God's grace and our efforts to grow in faith.

    - "It is God who is at work in you, enabling you . . ." (v. 13) Ask: **How do you know that God is at work within you? In what aspects of your life can you accept this truth?** Mention that we don't have to be perfect or whole for God to work in us and through us. The spiritual journey involves opening to and trusting God's presence within us.

    - "Work out your own salvation. . ." (v. 12) Indicate that this phrase refers to our small but essential role. Point out that we are not talking about salvation by works. It's not work "for" or work "up" your salvation but work *out* (make real, embody) the salvation that is already ours as a gift of grace in Christ Jesus. We work out our salvation by cooperating with God's saving, sanctifying grace at work in us.

    - Spiritual disciplines are practices that help us cooperate with God to work out our salvation. They help us pay attention to God's presence and call in our lives.

6. *Examine three metaphors of spiritual discipline*

- Offer the following metaphors as ways of viewing spiritual-life practices:
  - *Wind and sail.* The sail does not make a sailboat go; the wind powers the boat forward only as the sail is unfurled, allowing the wind to fill it.

LEADER NOTE/EXPANDED OPTIONS

Spiritual disciplines are little gestures of love by which we open our hearts and become available to the ever-active wind of God's Spirit blowing through our lives. With the help of meditation, prayer, scripture reading, acts of service, worship, and other practices, we allow the love of Christ to catch us up, fill and stretch us, and move our lives forward.

  - *A trellis.* A trellis does not "grow" a tomato vine, but it helps the vine grow by providing support for what the plant already wants to do. Likewise, patterns of spiritual practice provide support for the spiritual growth God wants to give us.

LEADER NOTE/EXPANDED OPTIONS

Through a regular pattern of intercessory prayer and acts of service, we might pray that God would give growth to the seed of forgiveness and compassion in us toward others. As we do our part in providing support to the Spirit's work through spiritual discipline, God nourishes in us the fruit of the Spirit for which the world hungers. What patterns of commitment give shape to your life? How are they life-giving?

• *Creating space.* Part of building a campfire is creating a space for it. God is building a fire in our hearts—at the center of our being—for which we must create adequate space and to which we must regularly attend.

LEADER NOTE/EXPANDED OPTIONS

God gives form to our lives as we clear out and maintain space for God to be God at the center of our being. Observing sabbath time is one of the chief ways to create space for attending to God in our days (a quiet time), weeks (Sunday worship), months (a sabbath day), and years (annual spiritual life retreats). To create space for God is to attend to God's presence and to let the Spirit empty us of all that gets in the way.

• Discuss briefly each metaphor and how it describes the spiritual disciplines.

  • Invite participants to identify which metaphor they find most helpful.

  • Ask if they remember the six spiritual disciplines being introduced in *Exploring the Way*. See how many they recall without looking. Remind them that the practices are listed on page 18 in Week 1 of the Participant's Book.

Invite class members to stand and stretch for two minutes and to help you rearrange chairs for paired sharing.

TASTE AND SEE (20 MINUTES)

Set a context.

The spiritual discipline we want to focus on today is sharing our spiritual journeys with one another. We acknowledge the general value in Christian fellowship, but perhaps we've never really thought about sharing our faith journeys as a spiritual discipline. Two elements of discipline come to the fore as we tell our stories:

• **First, we learn to talk about our spiritual lives with others, an activity we may feel reluctant to pursue despite its importance to growth in Christian community and witness.**

- **Second, we share part of our sacred journeys as a way to help others learn to pay closer attention to God's work in their own lives.**

Invite paired sharing.

Ask people to spend twelve to fifteen minutes sharing in pairs from the notes they jotted down in response to the two questions asked earlier *(questions on newsprint and page 21 of the Participant's Book)*:

- When have I undergone a positive change in my relationship with God or felt a new sense of adventure in my faith life?
- What spiritual practices or gifts have helped me in this shift?

Reflect as a class.

Take several minutes to reflect together on what it was like to share spiritual journeys in this way. Ask: **Can you think of ways to use this practice in your life? In what ways do you already practice this discipline?**

CLOSING (5 MINUTES)

Read a brief scripture text. Consider repeating Jeremiah 6:16 from the "Opening."

Sing a chant or song, or listen to a recorded song. (optional)

Invite participants into the week ahead.

Remind the class to make the most of the coming week by reading the Participant's Book and doing at least two or three of the spiritual exercises on sharing life journeys with others, followed by brief journaling.

Offer a benediction from Philippians 2:13.

As we go out let's remember: "It is God who is at work in [us], enabling [us] both to will and to work for [God's] good pleasure." Amen.

Week 3
Bread for the Journey

PREPARATION

Pray for the class and each person in it. Pray for a listening spirit and fresh insight as you prepare to teach. Pray also for a hospitable heart and centeredness in God's presence as you lead the class.

Review the entire class process. Select appropriate songs or hymns for both "Opening" and "Closing." Select some scripture references for the exercise under "Launching into the Depths," and preprint those on newsprint. Have some extra Bibles available. Prepare other newsprint or PowerPoint materials as needed.

Read "Setting the Stage" carefully, underlining sections you wish to emphasize. Be ready to put the basic ideas into your own words and to expand or adapt material based on your own experience and illustrations.

Expanded Class Options: To build a ninety-minute session, draw from the materials that appear in boxes. They may be added to enrich "Setting the Stage" or used to help people expand their understanding of prayer following the "Taste and See" experience. Use your discretion to shape class time.

Prepare the space before class begins. Near the center of the teaching space, set a small table with a cloth and candle as a focal point for worship and reflection.

OPENING (5 MINUTES)

Welcome the class, creating a warm and relaxed tone.

Set a context for this week's theme and spiritual practice.

This week we continue our exploration of the spiritual journey by talking about the role of meditation on scripture as a powerful means of spiritual formation. We will

experience the practice of *lectio divina,* or praying with scripture, as a way to be attentive to God's living word.

Join together in worship.

- *Light the candle, and say, "We light this candle as a reminder of Christ's presence with us."*
- *Sing a song: "Thy Word" or a song of your choosing.*
- *Read John 8:31-32.*

    Jesus says, "If you make my word your home, you will indeed be my disciples, you will learn the truth and the truth will make you free" (JB).

- *Lead a brief prayer.*

SHARING INSIGHTS (10 MINUTES)

Ask: **Can you name something that has happened this week related to learning from the last class or from the week's exercises?** Allow time to share insights or questions arising from the week's practice of sharing spiritual journeys with others and/or reading in the Participant's Book.

SETTING THE STAGE (15 MINUTES)

1. *Review.*

    Last week we explored the role of spiritual disciplines in our lifelong adventure of being on the spiritual journey. We learned that spiritual disciplines are a means of keeping our inner ear inclined toward God, of attending to God's presence and call in our lives. We practiced that last week through the discipline of sharing our spiritual journeys with one another as a way of paying attention to God. We are a means of grace to one another as we help each other pay attention to God's presence and receive the gifts of life that God gives us.

    Another great gift for our spiritual journey is the Bible. The Bible is a means of grace insofar as it enhances our awareness of God's presence, purpose, and power in our lives. The spiritual discipline that can sustain us on our spiritual journeys is regular meditation on scripture—listening to God's word for our lives through the Bible.

LEADER NOTE

Reading the Bible is a means of listening to God's Word.

What do we mean by God's Word? What does it mean to call these writings God's Word? The term *Word* has rich connotations:

- It is an expression of God's self-revealing, a means for communicating divine truth to us (just as we communicate and reveal ourselves to others in words)

- "The Word of God is the action of the presence, the purpose, and the power of God in the midst of human life."[1]

- The Word of God is fully present in Jesus and active through the Holy Spirit. (John 1:14, "The Word became flesh and lived among us"; Ephesians 6:17, "the sword of the Spirit, which is the word of God")

---

2. **Gregory the Great's image of scripture—the shallows and the depths**

   Gregory the Great, who was pope from 590–604, left behind a substantial literary heritage. In his popular commentary on the Book of Job, he compared the scriptures to a river, "broad and deep, shallow enough here for the lamb to go wading, but deep enough there for the elephant to swim."[2] His metaphor suggests that in the "open shallows" of the Bible, even children can find clear meaning; yet in the deeps of scripture, spiritual riches lie hidden that awe the minds of the greatest theologians.

   (On newsprint, sketch the simple diagrams below. Participants may draw the diagram in the space given in their outline on page 31 of the Participant's Book. In the first, the river has shallow edges and a deep center; the second depicts a cross section of a river with the water's surface and the riverbed dropping away from the shoreline.)

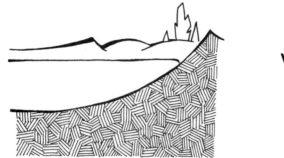 

Swimming in the Shallows

The shallows are meaningful. In the shallow of the river, we learn to get into the water; we learn to trust what's beneath the surface—that there is a bottom; we learn how to float, how to swim; we learn the gift and the dangers of water. But to stay only in the safety of the shallows, never to venture out into the depths or at least go fishing there, is to miss out on the full gift and wonder of what the river offers us.

Informational Approach to Scripture

The shallows represent the realm of information where we learn the following:
- **what is in the Bible, the stories and verses**
- **what the writers meant to communicate to the readers of their day**
- **where the biblical material came from**
- **customs and traditions**
- **how scriptures have informed doctrine and values**
- **general lessons or applications we might draw for our lives today**

This important background prepares us for a deeper encounter.

[Leader may elaborate here with more information from Leader Note on next page.]

LEADER NOTE

An example of information leading to formation:

> When I learned that women in Jesus' time did not receive religious instruction at the feet of the rabbis, I began to grasp Mary's courage in choosing to sit at Jesus' feet to listen to him (Luke 10:38-42). My image of Mary as the irresponsible little sister who thoughtlessly left Martha to do all the serving changed. The pictures I receive from responsible biblical scholarship greatly enrich my deeper reflection on God's word to me in my current life.[3]

Here you might share an example of your own. How did your knowledge *about* a passage of scripture facilitate your knowledge *of* scripture—help you to apply it to your own life in a personal way?

Launching into the Depths

The realm of the depths is the realm of formation. As we move into the formational realm:

- **We take that longest of journeys from the head to the heart, from knowledge about God to knowledge of God in our own experience.**

- **We move from a focus on studying the Bible to a primary interest in listening for God's voice.**

- **We move from trying to master the text to letting it master us, from grasping its meaning to letting ourselves be grasped by it.**

- **We move from seeing the Bible as a source of answers to a place of meeting and conversing with God.**

[If time allows, add more information from the box below, and/or ask the two questions with responses.]

LEADER NOTE/EXPANDED OPTIONS

Launching into the depths: moving from knowledge about *to knowledge of God*

If we want a real relationship with the living God, we need to go beyond intellectual engagement to meditating on God's Word. We can pray with the psalmist that "the meditation of my heart" will be acceptable to the Lord (Ps. 19:14). Meditating on, or praying with, the Bible differs from study.

- It is a way of listening to God through the words of scripture. The question behind the listening is this: How is God addressing me personally, right now, in this passage?

  [Refer to "Jim's Story" (page 35, Participant's Book) as an illustration they can read this week.]

- When we listen, we do not control the text or the message; we aren't trying to wrestle meaning or mine some gem of wisdom from it.

- We stand before the Word with an open mind and heart, vulnerable to the mystery of God; this requires us to be quiet and still within.

- We expect the Spirit to speak not what we *want* to hear but what we *need* to hear; we expect to be addressed, challenged, guided, assured, and changed.

Ask:

- **What do you associate with the shallows? What causes you to get stuck in the shallows?** *(Allow time for responses.)*

- **What do you associate with the depths? What helps you find the depths?** *(Allow time for responses.)*

The purpose of going into the depths is not just to know more about God but to come to know the God of the scripture in a more fully personal relationship.

Let's explore the meaning of God's Word in a more personal sense.

- Everyone take a Bible and find a favorite passage. Read the passage, and think for a moment about why it is a favorite passage of yours and what made it so. *(Allow time.)* [Post on newsprint some references for those who might have trouble finding a passage on their own: Psalm 23; Matthew 11:28-30; Philippians 4:6-7; Joshua 1:9; Isaiah 41:10; Hebrews 12:1-2]

- In the silence, imagine that Jesus is here. He wants to tell you that your association with that passage is no accident. He wants to share with you what God has always desired you to hear through that passage. Listen to what he says. Jot down what you hear in your heart. *(pause)* What do you want to say back to him? Write it down if you like. *(pause)*

- Share with someone sitting next to you what came to mind, what you heard, how you responded. *(pause)*

- What was that exercise like? *(Invite responses.)*

- What would you say it means to listen for God's Word in and through scripture? *(sharing in the whole group)*

3. Meditating on the Word is a way of making scripture our home.

- Jesus says, "'If you make my word your home you will indeed be my disciples, you will learn the truth and the truth will make you free'" (John 8:31-32, JB).

Lectio divina (pronounced lex-ee-oh div-ee-nah), or "holy reading," is one way of meditating on scripture from the Christian tradition that can help us make the word our home.

Lectio divina is basically reading, repeating, digesting, and contemplating small portions of scripture as food for the soul and as a form of prayer.

Some version of *lectio* has been practiced from the earliest centuries of the church's life through the present day. It started with the ancient Jewish practice of meditating on God's law (Torah) and was given a central place in Saint Benedict's monastic rule of life (sixth century). It received a four-stage form in the twelfth century, then threaded its way to us.

Now we'll spend a little time dwelling in God's word through meditation.

TASTE AND SEE (20 MINUTES)

Lead a guided *lectio* process, using Psalm 127:1-2 as the text. Follow instructions below (total time: approximately twelve minutes). Be sure participants know they are free to "pass" at any stage of sharing and that silence can be uncomfortable if they are not accustomed to experiencing it in a group. Encourage them with no pressure just to try it out.

Guide an experience of lectio divina.

Begin by reading an illustration of what it is like to pray the scriptures in this way. Say: **Here is how one man likens his experience of praying scripture** *(lectio divina)* **to reading a message from his wife.** Refer the group to "A Note on the Door" (pages 33–34, Participant's Book). Read this story aloud. Point out that the steps involved in the process of meditating on scripture are not unlike the process that Steve went through as he sought to understand a note from his wife.

Explain briefly the four steps of the process you will use for the *lectio divina* experience, writing the four *R* words below on newsprint. Then begin the exercise with a moment of silence, allowing time for participants to center themselves and to acknowledge God's presence.

(1) *READ* Psalm 127:1-2 slowly, inviting them to hear the verses as though for the first time. Ask them to voice a word or phrase that stands out for them.

(2) Read again, asking them to *REFLECT/meditate* on what thoughts/questions/feelings these words stir up in their minds or hearts. Say: **Choose a phrase and "chew on it." What does it mean to you? What would it mean for you to say it, to mean it, to pray it? What do you fear? How does this psalm address your fears?**

(3) Read a third time, inviting them to *RESPOND to God in prayer.* Ask them to remember and imagine that God is present and to respond to God personally with whatever is on their heart as they hear it read this time. Encourage them to write if it helps. *(pause)* Then ask them to listen in quietness to how God might respond to them in turn or what grace God might give them that they need. *(pause)*

(4) Read a final time. Invite them to *REST in God's presence* and in the confidence of these words. *(pause)* Ask them to say aloud to God a word of thanks for whatever gift they have received.

Form smaller groups and ask participants to respond to these questions about the experience *(write the questions on newsprint and post)*:

- What about that experience did you find helpful? difficult?
- What bread for the journey did you receive?

Gather the class together. Discuss what it means to make *lectio divina* a spiritual discipline; that is, an ongoing practice in one's life. **Meditating on scripture is a lifestyle— a way of living with the word, abiding in the word daily, cultivating a listening heart. It is a way of inclining one's ear and heart to God every day through a few minutes of *lectio*, meditating upon and praying with scripture.**

- Point class to "A Process for Personal *Lectio Divina*" (Participant's Book, page 36); tell them that these steps can guide them in a personal experience of *lectio divina*.

CLOSING (5 MINUTES)

Remind the class to make the most of the coming week by reading the Participant's Book and doing at least two or three of the spiritual exercises on *lectio divina* with further journaling.

Sing a hymn or song.

Close with a benediction:

Jesus said, "'If you make my word your home you will indeed be my disciples'" (John 8:31, JB). Let us go forward into this week, determining to dwell in God's Word and to let God's Word dwell in us. Amen.

Week 4
Drink for the Journey

PREPARATION

Pray for the class and each person in it. Pray for a listening spirit and fresh insight as you prepare to teach. Pray also for a hospitable heart and centeredness in God's presence as you lead the class.

Review the entire class process. Select songs for the "Opening" and "Closing" and a closing benediction. Find a chime or bell for the "Taste and See" experience. Prepare newsprint or PowerPoint materials as needed.

Read "Setting the Stage" carefully, underlining sections you wish to emphasize. Be ready to put the basic ideas into your own words and to expand on points with your own experience, ideas, stories, or illustrations. Adapt the material to fill the group's time commitment.

Expanded class options: To build a ninety-minute session, draw from the materials that appear in boxes. Use your discretion to shape class time.

Prepare the space before class begins. Near the center of the teaching space, set a small table with a cloth and candle as a focal point for worship and reflection.

OPENING (5 MINUTES)

Welcome the group, creating a warm and relaxed tone.

Set a context for this week's theme and spiritual practice.

> **This week we continue to explore our spiritual journeys by considering the role of prayer in our spiritual formation. Prayer gives us a way to pay attention to God in daily life. Indeed, prayer connects us to God and provides refreshment for our spiri-**

tual thirst. We'll be experiencing a particular method of prayer called breath prayer as one way to practice the presence of God.

Join together in worship.

- **We begin our time together by lighting this candle and becoming attentive to God's presence with us here and now.**

- *Read Romans 8:26.*

   Likewise the Spirit helps us in our weakness; for we do not know how to pray as we ought, but that very Spirit intercedes with sighs too deep for words.

- *Sing one verse of "Spirit of the Living God" or another song of your choosing.*

- *Offer a short prayer.*

SHARING INSIGHTS (10 MINUTES)

Allow participants to share insights or questions arising from their week's practice of *lectio divina* or their reading and reflection from the Participant's Book.

SETTING THE STAGE (10 MINUTES)

1. Review: **Last week we explored meditation on scripture as a spiritual practice that takes us beyond the usual limits of Bible study. Meditating is a way of regularly pondering and listening to the word. As we listen for God's voice in scripture, we become more familiar with the sound of God's voice in our lives and our hearts.**

2. **Another great gift for our spiritual journey, closely related to meditation, is prayer. Prayer is a means of grace that opens our minds and hearts to the living God. Many great spiritual writers tell us that prayer is the chief means of grace.**

   Address the centrality of prayer:

   - **Prayer is essentially our attention and openness to God, the fundamental inward orientation to God that grounds all fruitful spiritual practice and Christian living.**

   - **We can't mature into the fullness of Christ without prayer, and learning to pray requires practice.**

LEADER NOTE

Assumptions behind authentic prayer:

- *That as human beings we have the capacity to pray.* Since we are made in the image and likeness of God, we are deeply connected to God by the goodness of creative grace.

- *That we have a desire to communicate and relate to a deeply personal God.* This desire is also planted deep in our hearts by God's grace.

- *That God loves us; desires our company; and cares to speak to us, guide us, and provide for our needs.* Does our image of God allow us to embrace this truth?

---

3. **Examine our typical experience with prayer.**

Prayer is an aspect of our faith life we often take for granted.

- **Maybe we believe in the value of prayer, but we don't actually pray very much. Theoretically we know it's a good thing, but practically it poses problems.** Ask participants to share problems they've encountered (unsure of praying "right"; hard to squeeze prayer time into a busy day).

- **Our problem with prayer goes deeper than a scheduling issue. We suffer from what some writers (Parker Palmer, W. Paul Jones) call "functional atheism." Intellectually we believe in God, but practically we often act as if God were asleep or disinterested instead of a real, active presence in our lives and world.**

Our typical way of viewing prayer leaves us with many unanswered questions.

- We mostly think of prayer as talking to God, often asking for what we want. (Comedian Flip Wilson: "I'm gonna pray now; anyone want anything?")

- Then we wonder why some prayers are answered and others apparently not. This can create a faith crisis. What do we believe when our prayers "don't work"?

- As a result of these questions, we sometimes don't feel connected at all with God in prayer. We wonder if God is really there, if God cares, or if we're praying "right." We may feel too insignificant for God to bother with.

EXPANDED OPTIONS

Read the three "Quotes for Further Reflection" about prayer (page 47, Participant's Book).

- Ask which one people most resonate with and why.

- Invite responses; build on their thoughts and insights.

---

4. *Paint the larger picture of prayer*

Prayer is far more than asking for what we want.

- **"Beseeching the Lord" is one dimension of prayer. Jesus says, "Ask, and it will be given you; . . . how much more will your Father in heaven give good things to those who ask him!" (Matt. 7:7, 11).**

- **Seeking what we desire from God, while legitimate, is not the primary aspect of prayer.**

- **Look at the prayer Jesus taught his disciples.** (Post Lord's Prayer on newsprint.)

- *Ask:* **What key dimensions does Jesus include in the Lord's Prayer?** (Invite responses.) Keep the following points in mind:

  (1) It begins with adoration, praise, a commitment to God's purposes, and an offer to be part of what God wills for this world.

  (2) It calls us to forgive others so we might know the fullness of God's forgiveness for us.

  (3) It ends by affirming God's reign.

Jesus teaches us that prayer is about

  (1) paying close and reverent attention to God: "hallowed be your name,"

(2) asking for what *God* wants: "your kingdom come,"

(3) and seeking the grace we need to be part of what God is doing: "give us this day our daily bread . . . forgive us . . . rescue us."

LEADER NOTE/EXPANDED OPTIONS

Prayer is a relationship of growing, deepening communion with our Creator.

- Read slowly and gently through the quote by Flora Wuellner called "The Door of Prayer" (page 41, Participant's Book). Invite participants to name the phrase or sentence they would underline and why.

- Like any intimate relationship, prayer requires humble, truthful, loving communication.

- Communication runs two ways—listening as well as speaking. The closer we draw to God, the more we discover the importance of listening in our communication.

How do we listen to God? Ask this question and elicit responses from the class/group. Get a volunteer to write answers on newsprint/board. Keep in mind the following responses:

- Through the book we call God's Word; in nature; in the words/acts of others; in circumstances and "coincidences"; in the "still small voice" within our hearts.

- In silence: a quiet atmosphere is crucial to good listening, although God can get our attention even in a crowd! (discuss difficulties of finding/creating silence)

- Outer silence helps us pay attention, but we need to quiet our noisy thoughts as well. This isn't easy. Full of distractions and "inner noise," we find it hard to focus on God's presence. Many prayer practices aim to help us quiet the mind (thoughts) and still the heart (feelings) so we can listen clearly to God's voice.

Prayer is an openness to God's gracious presence in our world, at work in our lives

- **Prayer is a gift, not something we have to manufacture or initiate.** Read Romans 8:26, which states: "Likewise the Spirit helps us in our weakness; for we do not know how to pray as we ought, but that very Spirit intercedes with sighs too deep for words."

- **Prayer begins with God—the gift of God's presence. Prayer encourages a personal response to the presence of the Holy Spirit already active in our lives. Even when we do not know how to pray, the Spirit prays in us. God is the primary actor.**

- **Henri J. M. Nouwen once distinguished between "big *P* prayer" and "little *p* prayer." "Big *P* prayer" is God's Spirit praying in us. "Little *p* prayer" is what we do to make space for God's Spirit in and among us—to be open; to receive the grace, call, or guiding word God would give us.**

TASTE AND SEE (20 MINUTES)

Introduce the breath prayer (5 minutes).

We have time to learn and briefly practice a particular form of prayer many Christians find helpful in daily life. It is called breath prayer. The breath prayer is based on an early form of prayer in the Christian tradition called the Jesus Prayer.

(1) **The most common form of the Jesus Prayer is "Lord Jesus Christ, Son of God, have mercy on me, a sinner."**

(2) **This prayer was repeated many times each hour as a way to "pray unceasingly" and to keep remembrance of Jesus before each believer. The prayer gradually moved from the head to the heart, where the Spirit continued it inwardly.**

LEADER NOTE

The Jesus Prayer combines two confessions:

1. the most ancient confession of faith among early Christians ("Jesus is Lord")
2. the confession of sin spoken by the publican (tax collector) in Luke 18:13: "God, be merciful to me, a sinner!"

Breath prayer is a contemporary version of this ancient prayer form.

- **It is a short prayer phrase that can be carried in our memory through the day.**
- **It is a prayer of the heart, a deep desire before God that may express our prayer for many years as we mature in Christ.**
- **It is called "breath prayer" because the Hebrew word for breath, wind, and spirit are one; also, because it can become as natural as breathing.**

Review the basic method for finding a personal breath prayer ("Discovering Your Breath Prayer," Participant's Book, pages 44–45).

Encourage selecting the deepest and broadest prayer, if more than one comes to mind.

Practice the breath prayer (10 minutes)

- Allow participants to discover or select their prayer. (2 minutes)
- Invite them to become familiar with their prayer, to carry it with them while walking or to sit with it in quiet until you ring the chime or bell. (8 minutes)

Share the experience of finding and using a breath prayer (5 minutes)

Invite class members to talk about the process of finding their prayer and their experience of praying it. They need not share the specific prayer unless they wish. Offer affirmation and respond to questions. A few points:

- There is no right or wrong prayer; only deeper, more authentic prayer.
- Breath prayer may be used in many settings and activities.

- Notice how awareness of God's presence/guidance comes as we use the prayer; how it changes our perspective on ordinary things
- Breath prayer forms a bridge between prayers of asking and our listening. It draws us deeper into relationship with God, the true essence of prayer.

Closing (5 minutes)

Remind the group to make the most of the coming week by reading the Participant's Book and doing several of the spiritual exercises with prayer and further journaling.

Sing "Breathe on Me, Breath of God" or another song of your choosing.

Close with a benediction.

Week 5
Companions on the Way

PREPARATION

Pray for the class and each person in it. Pray for a listening spirit and fresh insight as you prepare to teach. Pray also for a hospitable heart and centeredness in God's presence as you lead the class.

Review the entire class process. Select appropriate songs or hymns for both "Opening" and "Closing" and a benediction for the "Closing." Prepare newsprint or PowerPoint materials as needed. You will need a bell or chime for the "Holy Listening" exercise. Make copies of the "Holy Listening" handout that appears at the end of this Leader's Guide session. You will be distributing this handout for use during the "Taste and See" portion of the meeting. This information differs from what appears in the Participant's Book.

Read "Setting the Stage" carefully, underlining sections you wish to emphasize. Be ready to put the basic ideas into your own words and to expand on any portions with your own experience, ideas, stories, or illustrations.

Expanded class options: To build a ninety-minute session, draw from the materials that appear below in boxes. Use them to enrich "Setting the Stage" or to expand learners' understanding after the "Taste and See" experience. Use your discretion to shape class time.

Prepare the space before class begins. Near the center of the teaching space, set a small table with a cloth and candle as a focal point for worship and reflection.

About Week 6: Tell the group that the last session of *Exploring the Way* will require 15–20 more minutes than usual. Make arrangements now for a longer meeting next week.

OPENING (5 MINUTES)

Welcome the class, creating a warm and relaxed tone.

Set a context for this week's theme and spiritual practice.

This week we continue to explore the spiritual journey by talking about the gift of companionship we have in one another. Our practice will be that of "holy listening," learning to listen deeply to each other.

Join together in worship.

- *Light the candle and say,* **We begin our time together by lighting this candle and becoming attentive to God's presence with us here and now.**

- *Sing a song: "Blest Be the Tie That Binds."*

- *Read 1 Corinthians 12:12-14, 27.*

  Just as the body is one and has many members, and all the members of the body, though many, are one body, so it is with Christ. For in the one Spirit we were all baptized into one body—Jews or Greeks, slaves or free—and we were all made to drink of one Spirit.

  Indeed, the body does not consist of one member but of many...

  Now you are the body of Christ and individually members of it.

- *Offer a brief prayer.*

SHARING INSIGHTS (5 MINUTES)

Invite participants to share briefly insights or questions arising from the past week. Ask, **What has happened this week that you can relate to learning from the last class or from the week's exercises on prayer?** Allow several to share within the shorter five-minute time frame. ("Sharing Insights" is shorter because the "Taste and See" portion requires more time today. If you meet for more than one hour, you may allow more time here.)

SETTING THE STAGE (20 MINUTES)

1. *Review:* **Last week we explored prayer as a means of grace that opens our minds and hearts to the living God. We discovered and practiced our breath prayer, a way to**

pray "unceasingly" through the day. This week we will see how being attentive to one another can help us be attentive to God's presence.

2. Community offers us an essential gift for the Christian spiritual journey.

- **God gives us an incredibly valuable gift in one another; we are by nature incomplete without this gift. We are "means of grace" to one another—a means by which God comes to us, touches us, and encourages us.**

- Ask: **How do you experience the gift of others?**

LEADER NOTE/EXPANDED OPTIONS

First Corinthians 12:12 reminds us that we are "all the members of the body" of Christ. The image of the body of Christ, our being members of one another, shows that only in relation to one another can we be complete and be who God intends us to be in love. The African word *ubuntu* (oo-boon-too) means "I am because we are." This word acknowledges our dependence upon one another. We exist as individuals because we sustain one another within our tribes, our families, our faith communities, and even our work units. The deepest wisdom of our faith is that the very nature of God is community: the Holy Trinity, one God in three Persons. What would it mean to live with such an understanding of our connectedness in Christ? (*Allow brief responses.*)

- **God did not intend that we travel life's path alone, particularly not the path of Christian discipleship. The Bible affirms the importance of companionship. Where do you see this in scripture?**

LEADER NOTE

In the book of Genesis God says "it is not good" for Adam to be alone. Humans need helpers, companions on the way in order to live faithfully as God's sons and daughters, stewards of creation. In Luke's Gospel (10:1), Jesus sends the apostles out in pairs—not alone. The bottom line: we are integrally connected to one another. Our wholeness and effectiveness depend on connection, relationship, community.

See Leader Note/Expanded Options at the end of Session 5 in this Leader's Guide for further information about faith communities.

---

3. Why is a community of believers important to spiritual growth?

- *Community teaches us the interdependence of spiritual health and vitality.* **Some people imagine Jesus as the ultimate individualist, needing no one but God. But listen to Matthew 3:1-3** *(read aloud).* **Ask, Who prepared the way for Jesus?** *(Invite sharing.)* **Now, think for a moment about your own life. Who has prepared the way for your spiritual growth?** *(Allow a moment of quiet and then share.)*

- *Close friendships help us mature in faith.* **When Gabriel visits Jesus' mother, Mary, and she says yes to God's new life growing in her, she immediately goes to tell Elizabeth. The events in Mary's life excite the new life Elizabeth is carrying, and we see a wonderful model of spiritual friendship—encouraging the new life in one another and expecting God's promise to bear fruit.**

EXPANDED OPTIONS

Ask, **Who has encouraged new life in you?** *(Allow time for responses.)*

The example of Mary and Elizabeth may be harder for some men to relate to. The idea of close friendship between men can be difficult for men in our culture that values solo performance as a form of "strength." Use the following quote if you think men in your group would find it helpful:

> [Chuck] is in his thirties, accomplished in his job, a single parent, a faithful churchgoer. But when asked if men like him tend to have true friends, he noted, "I have a lot of acquaintances, and I've been in some wonderful Bible study groups, but as far as a close friend or a one-on-one relationship, no. It's been a struggle. I need something like that, but it's uncharted water to me."[1]

• *Authentic community is a safe place to share questions, struggles, hopes, joys.* **Superficial community is common in the church. Many people search from church to church, looking for communities of truth and grace—that is, honest seeking and acceptance in place of pretense and facade. Some find this community in Alcoholics Anonymous or other recovery groups. Others find it in covenant groups. Some never find it. Do you have or have you ever had this kind of fellowship? Where do you find such shared life?** *(Allow time for responses.)*

LEADER NOTE

First John 1:7 says that "If we walk in the light as he himself is in the light, we have fellowship with one another." What is fellowship? The Greek word is *koinonia* (pronounced koy-nohn-EE-ah), which means "sharing in common." We have a shared life together that is honest and accepting. In this kind of community we learn to live in the healing light of God rather than the darkness of hidden shame or sin.

- *We can help hold one another accountable to our spiritual commitments.* Accountability is a relationship of loving support, forgiveness, and encouragement, although some have experienced accountability as a negative experience characterized by harsh authority and criticism. Hebrews 10:24-25 describes accountability that is rooted and nurtured in loving relationship. *(Read Hebrews 10:24-25 aloud.)* Ask: **What words or phrases stand out for you?**

EXPANDED OPTIONS

Ask: **Who have you given permission to hold you accountable to your highest commitments? Who prays for your spiritual growth? Who are your encouragers as you aim to follow Jesus?** *(Allow responses.)* **Every one of us needs to cultivate relationships of accountability to make progress on this journey. John of the Cross once said, "We grow in faith only through the frail instrumentality of one another." There are some things we cannot do for ourselves.**

- *We learn to respect others and celebrate common ground.* Community is often where we meet the person with whom we have the most difficulty. Community challenges us to learn to forgive, to make space for personalities and perspectives different from ours. When Jesus comes into our lives, he always brings his friends with him—and they are rarely the ones we would choose for ourselves! Simon the Zealot had to learn to get along with Matthew the tax collector in order to share a common life as disciples of Jesus. In sharing life journeys and stories of faith, we discover our deepest common ground: God.

- *Spiritual community is a place to seek understanding for deep or disturbing spiritual experiences.* When Saul (Paul) experienced Jesus on the road to Damascus, he experienced extreme disorientation, blinded by the light. The Spirit sent Ananias to interpret his experience and guide the next steps in his journey of transformation (Acts 9:1-19). Many people today who have powerful spiritual experiences need someone to listen with openness and acceptance and to help interpret those experiences in the light of faith.

- *God often speaks to us through others.* God speaks to all of us most clearly through the person of Jesus—who he was and what he did. Just as God spoke through Jesus, God can speak to us through others and to others through us. When God speaks through us, our words may be simple but profound. Sometimes we perceive God's hand in the moment, and sometimes we recognize it later. Often those who speak never know they have been instruments. *(Invite personal examples of this from group.)*

Learning to listen well is crucial to faith formation and healthy group life—so important that we're going to try a simple exercise in listening to each other.

TASTE AND SEE (25 MINUTES)

Distribute copies of the "Holy Listening" handout that appears on pages 79–80 of this Leader's Guide.

Listening deeply to another person places us on sacred ground. The person to whom we attend is a child of God, made in the divine image. Moreover, God is present with us when we listen deeply to one of God's precious sons or daughters. So we can also listen for God as we listen to the other person. We can pay attention to how God is present for and through the other and how God is present to us personally in the time of listening.

Introduce the "Holy Listening" exercise (5 minutes)

- Explain the basic steps of the Holy Listening exercise, using the handout that you have given them.
- Give group members a chance to pair up and pull their chairs to a space apart in the room. With an uneven number, you may pair up with the extra person. (You will still need to track the time.)
- Remind them that you will ring a bell or chime at the halfway point so they can stop, answer the questions on the back of the handout, and then change roles.
- Say, **The question for the speaker to address is this: Where have I felt God's presence or absence most in the last week?** (The speaker does not have to answer both parts of the question unless time permits.)

Practice holy listening according to "The Process" on the handout (15 minutes).

Reflect on the exercise (5 minutes).

Invite the members to come back together to discuss briefly their experience as listener and speaker. What did they learn through this exercise? (They may refer to their notes on the back of the handout sheet.)

CLOSING (5 MINUTES)

Remind the class to make the most of the coming week by reading the Participant's Book and doing at least one or two of the recommended exercises with further journaling and to review the "Principles of Holy Listening" (pages 51-52, Participant's Book).

Offer a brief scripture reading: Hebrews 10:24-25.

Sing a hymn or song: "We Are One in the Spirit."

Close with a benediction.

Holy Listening

. . . .

*"Great healing and insight can come simply by spend-
ing time in the presence of someone who hears us out."*[2]

. . .

In this exercise you listen deeply to another person and share honestly. Remember that your speaking and listening always take place in God's loving presence.

AS THE SPEAKER

Take this time to talk honestly about how you have sensed God's presence or felt God's absence during the past week or so.

AS THE LISTENER

Practice listening with your heart as well as your head. Along with the meaning of the words spoken, what feelings or mood do gestures, manner, or voice convey? How does the speaker's feeling tone help you to interpret or understand the spoken words?

Feel free to nod, smile, or gesture in response, but try not to talk unless you are asking a clarifying question ("Did you mean . . . ?") or affirming with simple acceptance ("I see." "Ah." "Mmmm.")

THE PROCESS *(15 minutes)*

- Decide who will speak first. Take a moment to recall silently that you are in God's presence.
- Let the speaker talk and the listener listen for five minutes. (Chime will sound at end.)
- Take a minute at the chime to note on back of this handout how you felt in your role and what you discovered.
- Reverse roles. Speak and listen for another five minutes.
- Note, at the chime, words or phrases that describe what you felt and learned.
- Then take a few minutes to compare notes with your partner.

(OVER)

Holy Listening
REVIEW QUESTIONS

· · · · · · ·

FOR THE LISTENER

- When were you most aware of God's presence (in you, in the other person, between you) in the midst of the conversation?

- What was the greatest challenge of this experience for you?

FOR THE SPEAKER

- What was the gift of the conversation for you?

- When were you most aware of God's presence (in you, in the other person, or between you) in the midst of the conversation?

LEADER NOTES/EXPANDED OPTIONS

If your meeting lasts ninety minutes, you may choose to present more of this information below after the second point of the "Setting the Stage" portion.

Many forms of faith community are possible.

- *General Christian fellowship.* What we experience in our congregations in worship, study, fellowship, and ministry.

- *One-on-one relationships.* Examples include the following:

   Prayer partner—mutual relationship of prayer support

   Spiritual friendship—informal spiritual guidance, often mutual

   Spiritual mentor or guide—more formal arrangement for one person to guide or mentor another (also called spiritual direction)

- *Various kinds of small groups.* Ask: **What kinds of small groups can you name in your church? outside the church?** (examples: Bible study, mission groups, prayer groups, life-stage support groups, and so on.)

- *Family.* Ideally our families serve as a small group to support our spiritual formation. Family is to be a community of love, forgiveness, and mutual encouragement where we practice "being church" in the domestic setting. Ask: **What kinds of practices can a family undertake to support and encourage spiritual formation for each member?** (examples: devotion and prayer, reflection on the day's events—the "glads," "mads," and "sads"—asking where we saw God today). We recognize that family rituals can be life-shaping, especially as we look back on our lives.

- *Spiritual-formation groups.* The purpose of spiritual-formation groups is companionship with others who seek to grow in the fullness of Christ through honest reflection on life, regular spiritual practice, and encouragement for living out God's call. Spiritual-formation groups are not so much about supporting one another (though they do) as helping each member receive the support of the Spirit. The common focus is God's presence and call in our lives. *Companions in Christ* is an example of such a group. Covenant Discipleship groups serve a similar purpose for many.

Difficulties in Spiritual Companionship and Spiritual-Formation Groups

- *We may have anxiety about being "transparent" or vulnerable when sharing in a group or even with one other person.* It takes trust to share our deeper feelings, doubts, needs, and hopes. Trust can take time to develop and should never be rushed. Each person has his or her own pace; we should not be afraid to claim a pace that feels right. God is patient.

- *Matters of faith or spiritual experience may seem too personal to share.* Many of the older generations were taught that faith is a private realm. We must honor each person's sense of boundaries.

- *The time commitment required for meeting with another person or group seems too much.* The commitment of time can be difficult in our typically busy lives. This tension invites us to ask ourselves where our priorities lie, so we can weigh the costs and benefits of seeking deeper spiritual growth.

Week 6
Reaching Out in Love

PREPARATION

Pray for the class and each person in it. Pray for a listening spirit and fresh insight as you prepare to teach. Pray also for a hospitable heart and centeredness in God's presence as you lead the class.

Review the entire class process. Select appropriate songs or hymns for both "Opening" and "Closing." Prepare newsprint or PowerPoint materials as needed.

Since this is the last session, alert class members ahead of time that the "Closing" will require an extra fifteen to twenty minutes.

Read "Setting the Stage" carefully, underlining sections you wish to emphasize. Be ready to put the basic ideas into your own words and to expand on any portions with your own experience, ideas, stories, or illustrations.

Prepare the space before class begins. Near the center of the teaching space, set a small table with a cloth and candle as a focal point for worship and reflection.

OPENING (5 MINUTES)

Welcome the class.

Set a context for this week's theme and spiritual practice:

For these six weeks we've been learning to listen to God through various spiritual practices. All of these practices lead us to reach out and respond to the world that God loves. Today we explore a way of listening to God that leads us to the discovery of God's call in our lives to reach out to others.

Join together in worship.

- *Light the candle saying,* **Let's begin our time together by lighting this candle, reminding ourselves of God's presence.**

- *Sing one verse of "Breathe on Me, Breath of God," or a verse of a song of your choosing.*

- *Read Matthew 28:19-20:*

  > **"Go therefore and make disciples of all nations, baptizing them in the name of the Father and of the Son and of the Holy Spirit, and teaching them to obey everything that I have commanded you. And remember, I am with you always, to the end of the age."**

- *Offer a brief prayer.*

SHARING INSIGHTS (10 MINUTES)

Ask if anyone would like to tell about a holy listening experience from the week. Allow participants to share insights or questions arising from their week's practice of holy listening or any of their reading/reflection from the Participant's Book.

SETTING THE STAGE (20 MINUTES)

1. Introductory remarks

(Post newsprint with the five underlined portions in the list below printed on it.)

Our formation in Christ is "for the sake of the world," not merely for our personal well-being. Our class definition of spiritual formation ends with this phrase. Everything we have talked about and experienced over these six weeks leads us to listen to God's call and to act on that call in relation to the world.

- **We've learned how <u>journaling</u> helps bring us into conversation with God.**

- **We've experienced how <u>sharing our faith stories</u> reminds us of the constancy of God's love, presence, and calling in our lives.**

- **We've seen how <u>meditating on scripture *(lectio divina)*</u> helps us hear God's Word and sense God's call to us.**

- We've been invited into prayer, which deepens our relationship with the source of all life, and we have glimpsed how the <u>breath prayer</u> allows us to "pray without ceasing."

- We've practiced <u>holy listening</u> and seen how it encourages us to watch for God's tracings in the lives of others and God's activity in our own lives.

Today we will consider the question, Where is God calling us to reach out in love to be the presence of Christ in the world? As we continue learning to listen to God—today through the practice of the examen—we will explore how listening for God's call leads us to reach out to others.

- *God gives us a remarkable gift in the wider world.* Not only do we know the blessing of more intimate communities (family, friends, small groups), we are also part of a much larger community that offers both abundant resources and pressing needs. Together these form the context for our personal mission.

- *Each of us has a God-given purpose or mission in this life.* Christians name it as our "calling" from God, our vocation in the world. Any walk of life or profession can be the setting for living out our call.

- *Christian vocation is more than a religious call to ministry or mission work.* Our calling is to be fully available to God everyday. It involves hearing and responding to God's call in the midst of ordinary life.

2. *Listening deeply prepares us to respond faithfully.*

- *God's great refrain to Israel in the Bible is* to hear and obey (see Deut. 6:3). This phrase implies first listening with receptivity, then moving toward what is heard.

    Henri Nouwen, one of most beloved spiritual writers of the twentieth century, was fond of pointing out that the word *obedience* comes from the Latin root *audire*, which relates to hearing or listening.[1]

    [*Write the Latin word on board/newsprint*]

- *As we keep listening to the voice of God's love, we find our response shaped by this love.*

   Author Roberta Bondi reminds us we can't fully love God without loving God's *image*[2]: this includes you, the person next to you, and every other person—even enemies! Learning to love as God loves is challenging.

3. *Who are the neighbors Jesus invites us to reach out to?*

   - "This love of our neighbour is the only door out of the dungeon of self,"[3] said writer George MacDonald. Can we learn to see our neighbor's need as an invitation from Christ to lay down our life in some way?

   - We are challenged to see our neighbor as one worthy of equal regard and kindness as those near and dear to us—even if that neighbor seems foreign or strange. Remember, Jesus' story of the good Samaritan challenged the Jews of his day to see the much-hated Samaritans as possible neighbors.

   - Ask the group members to identify potential neighbors Jesus may be inviting them to love or reach out to. Gather responses on newsprint and expand on possibilities.

Invite the class/group to identify stories of Jesus' reaching out to those in his culture who

   - were not accepted by polite society (offer examples: prostitutes, tax collectors, lepers, persons outside the Jewish fold like the Samaritan woman at the well, or the Syrophoenician woman who showed much faith)

   - were not highly regarded within the Jewish social order (women and children)

Ask the class to return their attention to the newsprint list of their potential neighbors.

   - Invite a few minutes of quiet reflection on how each person might reach out to one such neighbor. If time permits, let a few people share their insights.

   - Then offer a brief prayer that our minds, hearts, and hands will be open to what God would have us do in a spirit of Christlike love.

4. *Moving from a sense of life work as career to life work as vocation (call)*

   Our life has a God-given purpose, and each of us has a personal mission in life.

   - **Our larger purpose is to glorify God by becoming fully human and alive in Christ (the undistorted image of God in a human being).**

   - **Our personal mission may take an infinite variety of forms while supporting this larger purpose.**

   - Invite the class to a moment of quiet reflection on their sense of personal mission in life and to jot down what comes to mind. **It has been said, "God doesn't call the qualified, but qualifies the called." Perhaps an illustration will encourage us.**

     One laywoman, pondering the invitation to lead a school of prayer and feeling inadequate to the task, confided her fears to a friend. Her friend said, "Don't be afraid. . . . God's desperate. God will use anybody." In a letter to her grandchildren years later, that woman wrote, "It is not the most brilliant that God uses. It is the most available, the most trusting, and the most faithful."[4]

   - **If we learn to listen to God consistently in daily life, we will hear the call that comes to us through little nudges, inner whispers, the words of another, or a sense of divine prompting in ordinary events and relationships.**

   - **Responding to this call can be called "practicing the presence of God" in daily life.**

5. *Practicing the presence of God in daily life*

   - Invite the class/group to think of times they have "practiced the presence of God" in everyday life (responding to an inner prompting or nudging of the Spirit at home, at church, in travel, with family members, friends, neighbors, colleagues, or strangers). You might "prime the pump" with a few examples of your own.

   - **One way to practice the spiritual discipline of self-examination or daily examen comes in recalling where we have sensed the call or prompting of the Spirit and how we have responded or not responded. This course has focused on learning to listen to God. As we learn to listen, we begin to discern where God is calling us to be Christ's presence in the world.**

- We're going to learn a little more about the daily examen and try one form of it. You can try other forms during the week ahead.

TASTE AND SEE (20 MINUTES)

The examen gives us a way to become more aware of our daily call to be fully available to God. Here is the form we will try together now.

Introduce the daily examen (5 minutes)

The Upper Room Dictionary of Christian Spiritual Formation defines *examen* as "A way of examining or assessing one's life before God on a regular basis." [5]

- Point out that the prayer of examen has two movements:
  - *Examination of consciousness*—reviewing how God has been present to us or at work with us through the day, then noting our response. This review helps us discern the "footprints" of the holy in daily life, and to gauge how we are attending and responding to God.
  - *Examination of conscience*—inviting God to search our hearts with the scrutiny of divine love, showing us what we need to see within, especially whatever is in need of cleansing, healing, forgiveness, and renewal.

- Make it clear to the group that the purpose of self-examination is diagnostic, not punitive. It helps us become more self-aware, to gain greater self-knowledge in relation to God's love.

Practice the daily examen (10 minutes)

- Point to the daily examen description (page 60, Participant's Book). Allow a minute for people to read the steps. Then invite the class members to try this form of self-examination for the next five minutes.

  Note: If your class meets in the morning or early afternoon, ask participants to review the last twenty-four hours; if you meet in the late afternoon or evening, have people review the day.

Reflect on the exercise (5 minutes)

- Invite class/group members to discuss their experience of this exercise and their learnings.

- Point out that the more we practice this daily pattern, the easier it becomes to remember and develop an awareness of the "God moments" or "divine calling cards" of your day.

- Move into the "Closing" by calling attention to the questions posted on newsprint and allowing some quiet time for reflection.

Closing (15 minutes—extra time needed)

After reflection time, invite class members to respond to these questions (posted on newsprint or PowerPoint):

- What has been most helpful about these six weeks together?

- Do you have a sense of a specific call from God?

- How might God be calling you—and us—to reach out to the world or to be the presence of Christ for others in some particular way?

- How will we continue exploring the way of the Christian spiritual life?

An Alternate Closing

Use the last examen from the Participant's Book Spiritual Exercises for the coming week, reprinted below. It is a way to review the six weeks in the form of the examen.

Say: **Examine the last six weeks of study, learning, and experience in Christian spiritual formation. Ask yourself these questions** (post on newsprint):

1. For what are you most grateful? What has been most enlivening or energizing?

2. For what are you least grateful? What has drained or tired you the most?

3. Based on your responses, what is the life-giving path God seems to be drawing you toward? How does this affect your sense of God's calling to you?

Allow time for sharing responses to these questions.

Remind the class to make the most of this final week by reading the Participant's Book and doing at least two or three of the recommended exercises with further journaling. Encourage people to continue practicing the spiritual disciplines they have learned.

Invite class members to sign up for some study beyond this six-week course. Encourage them to expand the journey they have begun and to continue exploring the life-giving way of Jesus Christ.

Offer specific options and perhaps sign-up sheets. You might include

- *Companions in Christ:* the foundational twenty-eight-week resource. *Exploring the Way* is intended to lead participants into this resource that will expand and deepen the spiritual practices this six-week course introduced. We highly recommend that *Exploring the Way* groups lead into a *Companions in Christ* twenty-eight-week group. Groups may choose to take breaks between the five parts of the longer resource.

- Other resources in the Companions in Christ series. These shorter (eight to ten weeks) resources include these titles: *The Way of Grace, The Way of Blessedness, The Way of Forgiveness.* We recommend that groups study them in this order.

- A book study on spiritual life practices such as Richard Foster's *Celebration of Discipline,* Marjorie Thompson's *Soul Feast,* or Maxie Dunnam's *The Workbook of Living Prayer.*

Offer a scripture reading: Matthew 28:19-20.

Sing a hymn or song.

Close with a charge and benediction.

> **Our formation in Christ is "for the sake of the world." Go forth from here to be the presence of Christ in the world! Amen.**

Glossary of Terms in Spirituality

Breath Prayer

"A short prayer of petition or praise that develops our awareness of God's presence."[1] Examples: "Holy Spirit, fill me." "Good Shepherd, guide my path." As a personal adaptation of the ancient Jesus Prayer (see below), breath prayer draws on the common meaning of "breath" and "spirit" in Hebrew. Christians understand that the Spirit prays in us as naturally as physical breath moves in us. The goal of this way of prayer is to "integrate interior thoughts with exterior actions."[2]

Centering Prayer

A method of praying based on ancient traditions in the church, including the early desert fathers and mothers and the fourteenth-century prayer classic *The Cloud of Unknowing*. This way of prayer helps to clear the mind of its ordinary "chatter" so that awareness of God can be sustained. Involving twenty minutes of silence both morning and evening, the purpose of Centering Prayer is to remove obstacles to contemplation.

Contemplation

The soul's focused attention on God in deep yearning for union with God's all-encompassing love. Thomas Merton defined contemplation as "resting in God by suspending activity, withdrawing into solitude, and allowing the intensity of Christ's love to work in the soul."[3] Merton felt sure that contemplation belongs to *all* Christians, not just to the great saints.

Discernment

The capacity to distinguish between truth and falsehood, in particular between human or demonic illusion and the prompting of the Holy Spirit. Generally, "to see, know, or understand the essence of a matter or inner nature of a person . . . by immediate and direct insight."[4] True discernment comes as a gift of grace, but we can prepare ourselves to receive it by various methods, including prayer, listening, and inward detachment from specific results.

Examen (or Examination of Conscience/Consciousness)

"A way of examining or assessing one's life before God on a regular basis,"[5] developed by Ignatius of Loyola (founder of the Jesuit Order). This form of prayer reviews a time span from a day to a week of our lives. Examination of consciousness helps us evaluate how God has been present and how we have responded, either faithfully or unfaithfully. Examination of conscience allows us to discover areas of our lives that need God's healing, forgiveness, and restoration.

Jesus Prayer

An ancient Christian prayer combining the earliest affirmation of the church ("Jesus is Lord") with the confessional prayer of the publican in Luke 18:13 ("God, be merciful to me, a sinner!"). The most common form is: "Lord Jesus Christ, Son of God, have mercy on me, a sinner." The prayer is repeated inwardly while meditating, working, or walking. It leads over time to the integration of the whole person—the mind being "recollected" in the heart and the heart being purified in loving obedience to God.

Journaling

The practice of keeping a written record of insights, feelings, questions, and prayers as they emerge from within us. Journaling helps us discover more fully who we are, allows us to track our spiritual growth over time, and enables us to integrate life experiences with deepening faith. We can journal with scripture passages, life circumstances, nature, and dreams.

Lectio Divina

Literally "divine reading" or "sacred reading," rooted in the ancient Hebrew practice of meditating on the Word of God. It is a way of encountering scripture not so much to inform the mind as to form the heart. *Lectio* cultivates deep listening to how God speaks personally to us through the Word, allowing "that Word to shape an appropriate response in thought, prayer, and the conduct of daily life."[6] The four classic phases of *lectio* in simple terms are these: Read, Reflect, Respond, and Rest.

Meditation

For Christians, meditation finds its roots in the ancient Hebrew practice of repeating short portions of the Torah with pauses in between. Repetition fosters a focus of attention that moves one "beyond thought to a wakeful presence to God."[7] In a general sense, meditation means pondering the things of faith—allowing words, meanings, and images to interact with thoughts, hopes, memories, and feelings—so that God can speak a living word to your current condition.

Monasticism

An expression of the Christian life that protects and sustains the individual quest for union with God through solitude, silence, and prayer. Present in many of the world's great religious traditions, monastic life in the Christian tradition allows for both solitary hermits and monks in community. Monastic vows typically include poverty, chastity, and obedience.

Mysticism

Human religious experience relating to the mystery of God. Human words and concepts cannot adequately describe mystical experience because it touches on God's holiness and transcendence—spiritual realities beyond our comprehension. While we cannot know all there is to know of God, we can by grace experience a depth of union with God through love. This is the essence of Christian mysticism, where union with God in love is known through Jesus Christ.

Retreat

Time set apart from ordinary life for the purpose of deepening one's relationship with God. A retreat can last for several hours, several days, or even several weeks. It is generally taken in a secluded setting to facilitate silence, solitude, prayer, and reflection. A rhythm of periodic personal retreats can greatly benefit spiritual growth. Many churches and retreat centers also offer group spiritual retreats that balance personal solitude with group reflection.

Sanctification

"The act and process of being made holy . . . in imitation of and participation in God's own holiness."[8] The New Testament stresses that our "ongoing transformation to 'Christlikeness'"[9] is essential to sanctification. Thus we can say with assurance that the doctrine of sanctification provides the Christian theological framework for understanding spiritual formation and for practicing spiritual disciplines (see below). The goal of sanctification is union with God.

Solitude

The common meaning is to be alone, but the spiritual meaning is oneness or unity of mind and heart. It is not necessary to be alone to experience solitude, although the quiet afforded by being alone makes it easier to experience genuine solitude. Oneness of mind and heart comes as we surrender our masks to God and listen deeply to the One who created us in the divine image. "Paradoxically, solitude actually enables us to connect to others in a far deeper way than does mere attachment to others."[10]

Spiritual Guidance

The guidance of the Holy Spirit in the lives of believers that comes in many ways. Broadly, the church offers spiritual guidance through preaching, teaching, counseling, and social witness. Spiritual guidance may also be offered within small groups committed to listening deeply to God and to one another. More specifically, spiritual guidance or direction occurs between two Christians as one seeks counsel from the other. Such counsel is not merely well-meaning advice or psychological counseling. It is the guiding counsel of the Holy Spirit sought through careful listening and prayerful attention.

Spiritual Disciplines

Basic practices of the Christian life that enable God to reshape our habits and transform us to greater Christlikeness. Disciplines are like garden tools; they can prepare the hard, rocky, weedy soil of our hearts to receive God's new life. They cannot, in themselves, guarantee healthy growth; but they make it more likely that grace can gain a firm foothold. Classic spiritual practices include prayer, fasting, charitable giving (alms), scriptural study and meditation, worship and sacrament, examination of conscience, and hospitality to strangers.

Spiritual Formation

The process of being reshaped according to the image of Christ by the gracious working of the Holy Spirit. This process is lifelong, for the Spirit carries us ever deeper into the reality of Christ. Christ reveals our true humanity to us, the image of God in human life that we too are created to bear. Our own formation in Christ is a witness to the reign of God in the midst of a deeply misshapen and broken world. Therefore spiritual formation cannot be understood apart from its relationship to the world God loves in Jesus Christ.

Spirituality

The way we live our Christian life with integrity; the pattern of our spiritual practice that gives particular shape to a faithful living witness. Some Christians express a more inwardly focused spirituality and some a more outwardly focused spirituality, but every authentically Christian spirituality will include a balance of interior practice and visible witness in the world. Christian spirituality is inherently holistic because Jesus embodied the complete integration of physical, spiritual, mental, emotional, and relational dimensions of human life, all united in divine love.

Upper Room Ministries
An Annotated Resource List

The following list contains information about books in the Companions in Christ series, books and resources that may be excerpted in *Exploring the Way*, and resources that expand on the material in this resource. As you read and share with your group, you may find some material that particularly challenges or helps you. If you wish to pursue individual reading on your own or if your small group wishes to follow up with additional resources, this list may be useful. Unless otherwise indicated, these books can be ordered online at www.upperroom.org/bookstore/ or by calling 1-800-972-0433.

THE COMPANIONS IN CHRIST SERIES

Companions in Christ: Participant's Book: A Small-Group Experience in Spiritual Formation by Stephen D. Bryant, Gerrit Scott Dawson, Adele J. Gonzalez, E. Glenn Hinson, Rueben P. Job, Marjorie J. Thompson, and Wendy M. Wright

Participants experience a deeper experience of God as they are guided through twenty-eight weeks of readings and exercises from well-known authors. The five parts of *Companions in Christ* include: Embracing the Journey (spiritual formation as a journey toward wholeness and holiness); Feeding on the Word (reading scripture in fresh ways); Deepening Our Prayer (various forms and styles of prayer); Responding to Our Call (serving God in willing obedience); and Exploring Spiritual Guidance (ways of giving and receiving spiritual guidance). Each part offers a range of spiritual practices to help sustain a lifelong ever-deepening faith journey.

#0-8358-0914-5

Companions in Christ: Leader's Guide: A Small-Group Experience in Spiritual Formation by Marjorie J. Thompson and Stephen D. Bryant

The Leader's Guide provides detailed outlines and material for leading each of the weekly

meetings. It also helps the leader identify and develop leadership qualities called upon when leading formational groups—qualities such as patience, trust, acceptance, and holy listening skills. The rich content brings a unique experience to each of the twenty-eight weeks.
#0-8358-0915-3

Companions in Christ: The Way of Grace (Participant's Book) by John Indermark
0-8358-9878-4
Companions in Christ: The Way of Grace (Leader's Guide) by Marjorie J. Thompson and Melissa Tidwell
0-8358-9879-2
The Way of Grace will delight small-group participants who find within its pages a fresh approach to the Gospel of John. This fourth release in the Companions in Christ series invites us to travel with eight biblical characters (or groups of characters) who discover God's grace through their encounters with Jesus. The resource is more than a survey of the biblical stories. It is a transforming interaction with the events and the characters. *The Way of Grace* invites us to open our hearts to a deeper knowing of God's grace.

Companions in Christ: The Way of Blessedness (Participant's Book)
by Stephen D. Bryant and Marjorie J. Thompson
#0-8358-0992-7
Companions in Christ: The Way of Blessedness (Leader's Guide) by Stephen D. Bryant
#0-8358-0994-3
The Way of Blessedness invites small-group members to discover and live in the values and the perspectives of the kingdom of God. Each week participants explore one of the Beatitudes from the Sermon on the Mount. The nine-week journey into Matthew 5 leads us through spiritual practices that can reshape our minds and hearts to resemble Christ more fully and empower us to live with Christ's love in this world.

Companions in Christ: The Way of Forgiveness (Participant's Book)
by Marjorie J. Thompson
#0-8358-0980-3
Companions in Christ: The Way of Forgiveness (Leader's Guide) by Stephen D. Bryant and Marjorie J. Thompson
#0-8358-0981-1
The Way of Forgiveness uses scripture meditation and other spiritual practices to guide us through an eight-week exploration of the forgiven and forgiving life. Always keeping God's grace and our blessedness before us, we examine shame, guilt, and anger before turning to forgiveness and reconciliation. This is powerful, challenging material with great transforming potential. It should be used by groups already bonded in trust and care for one another.

Journal: A Companion for Your Quiet Time
Introduction by Anne Broyles
Let the fresh, clean pages of *Journal* become an open invitation for endless faith discoveries as you record your creative ideas, reflections, and questions on passages of scripture, or personal prayers. The Upper Room *Journal* provides generous space for writing, faint lines to guide your journaling, and a layflat binding that helps to create a smooth writing motion. The margins of many pages contain inspirational thoughts to encourage your time of reflection.
#0-8358-0938-2

The Faith We Sing
A handy, portable feast of contemporary songs in a wide range of styles, this hymnal supplement is available in a variety of print editions and has a CD Accompaniment Edition as well. To see the full range of *The Faith We Sing* products or to place an order visit www.cokesbury.com or call 1-800-672-1789.

BEGINNING THE JOURNEY

A Seeker's Guide to Christian Faith by Ben Campbell Johnson
This Christian primer is for those who are asking the question "How can I experience God?" *A Seeker's Guide to Christian Faith* serves as a simple introduction to the most basic understandings of the Christian faith and will help new believers (and longtime believers too) begin the journey toward knowing God. In ordinary language, free from church jargon, the guidances are organized in six overarching themes, essential to the Christian faith: Getting Your Bearings, Naming Your Hunger, Learning a New Language, Discovering the Book, Expressing the Faith, and Reaching Farther.
#0-8358-0907-2

Seeker's Guide to Christian Faith Packet (10 books + free Leader's Guide)
#0-8358-0908-0

Heart Whispers: Benedictine Wisdom for Today by Elizabeth J. Canham
Heart Whispers offers insights from Benedictine spirituality to help us realize the need for faithful living and balance in today's stressful world. Readers will discover anew that life with God is a journey that grows richer and more blessed as we respond to divine grace. Leader's Guide (0-8358-0893-9) with ten sessions available.
#0-8358-0892-0

Invitation to Presence: A Guide to Spiritual Disciplines by Wendy J. Miller
For those who find the classical disciplines in church traditions a little stuffy and inaccessible, *Invitation to Presence* provides a user-friendly approach to the world of spiritual disciplines

based on Jesus' understanding of ministry. Miller encourages us to accept Jesus' invitation to "come and see" the stumbling blocks in our way, the disciplines available to us to remove these obstacles, and the work and presence of God in our lives. Miller's book can be used by individuals or small groups; a twelve-session leader's guide (#0-8358-0774-6) is also available.
#0-8358-0736-3

Journaling: A Spiritual Journey by Anne Broyles
In this revised and expanded edition of her best-selling book, Broyles offers new stories, guided meditations, and questions to help you enrich your relationship with God through spiritual writing. The book includes practical advice for journaling and sufficient space for practicing each of the six methods of journaling the author outlines. Appropriate for individuals or small groups, *Journaling* is an excellent aid for reflecting on your relationship with God and gaining insight into your unique walk of faith.
#0-8358-0866-1

The Workbook on Becoming Alive in Christ by Maxie Dunnam
This workbook presents material for daily reflection, along with material for group discussion, on the subject of the indwelling Christ as the shaping power of our lives as Christians. This seven-week small-group resource will deepen your understanding of the Christian life and what it means to mature in Christ. Dunnam believes that spiritual formation requires discipline and practiced effort to recognize, to cultivate an awareness of, and to give expression to the indwelling Christ.
#0-8358-0542-5

SHARING THE ADVENTURE

Discovering Community: A Meditation on Community in Christ by Stephen V. Doughty
Doughty kept a weekly appointment with his journal to answer the question, "Where this past week have I actually seen Christian community?" In his work with over seventy congregations, he found an abundance of times and places where he witnessed genuine community. Out of these experiences, he helps you understand what fosters Christian community and what blocks it. This resource can help to bring a renewed sense of personal calling and commitment to shared ministry for individuals and congregations.
#0-8358-0870-X

Remembering Your Story: Creating Your Own Spiritual Autobiography by Richard L. Morgan
Richard Morgan guides readers to understand and share their spiritual stories in *Remembering Your Story*. Morgan weaves insights from evangelism, Bible study, family therapy, pastoral care, gerontology, spiritual direction, and theology. He flavors his insights with illustrations from

poetry and fiction. His work guides us as individuals to discover the story of our spiritual journeys and to share those stories with others. Leader Guide (#0-8358-0964-1) available.
#0-8358-0963-3

BREAD FOR THE JOURNEY

Shaped by the Word: The Power of Scripture in Spiritual Formation, rev. ed., by M. Robert Mulholland Jr.
Shaped by the Word considers the role of scripture in spiritual formation and challenges you to move beyond informational reading to formational reading of the Bible. Mulholland demonstrates how your approach to scripture will in large measure determine its transforming effect upon your life. He examines the obstacles often faced in opening ourselves to God's living word. You will find this a helpful resource as you examine daily patterns of attentiveness to God through scripture, and you will expand your learnings about formational reading.
#0-8358-0936-6

Gathered in the Word: Praying the Scripture in Small Groups by Norvene Vest
Vest offers detailed guidelines for small groups to engage in a prayerful approach to scripture. The author presents this process in a creative way by giving instructions and then illustrating with a description of a small group that is using this approach to scripture. It is an excellent resource for groups that wish to pray the scriptures together.
#0-8358-0806-8

A Turbulent Peace: The Psalms for Our Time by Ray Waddle
Waddle helps us discover the comfort and the inspiration of the Psalms, particularly in light of the anxieties and stresses of living today. Waddle writes about each of the 150 Psalms. His meditations cause us to read each psalm for ourselves, to see these poems with new eyes, and to love them with fresh hearts.
#0-8358-9873-3

DRINK FOR OUR THIRST

Beginning Prayer by John Killinger
A basic resource for persons who are seeking to grow in their prayer life and develop a daily pattern of prayer. The book covers such subjects as attitudes that foster prayer, establishing daily prayer times, selecting a place for prayer, postures of prayer, and specific types of prayer.
#0-8358-0676-6

Creating a Life with God: The Call of Ancient Prayer Practices by Daniel Wolpert
This book offers the opportunity to learn and adopt twelve prayer practices. These prayer

practices include the general practice of peace and quiet, *lectio divina* (praying the scripture), the Jesus prayer, creativity, journaling, and more. Along with these prayer practices are historical figures to guide us. Some of these are Julian of Norwich, The Pilgrim (who prayed the Jesus Prayer), and Ignatius of Loyola. In addition to these helpful guides, Wolpert offers individuals and small groups step-by-step instructions for practicing each prayer practice.
#0-8358-9855-5

Dimensions of Prayer: Cultivating a Relationship with God by Douglas V. Steere
A classic on prayer, first published in 1962 and revised in this new edition published in 1997. Steere, in his warm and engaging style, writes about the basic issues of prayer—why we pray, what prayer is, how to pray, what prayer does to us and to our activity in the world. Tilden Edwards says that reading this book is like sitting at the feet of one the wisest spiritual leaders of the twentieth century and hearing what important things he has learned about prayer over a lifetime.
#0-8358-0971-4

The Workbook of Living Prayer by Maxie Dunnam
A six-week study on prayer. It includes material for daily readings and prayers with reflection suggestions. The tremendous popularity and widespread use of this workbook demonstrate its effectiveness in a variety of settings and attest to the essential, time-tested nature of its teachings about prayer. The author gives special attention to what we learn from Christ about the life of prayer.
#0-8358-0718-5

Responding to God: A Guide to Daily Prayer by Martha Graybeal Rowlett
This resource helps us understand prayer as a response to God's grace in our lives. This book and accompanying leader's guide contain a suggested model for daily prayer and material for ten weeks of study on the various facets of prayer. It includes chapters on our understanding of God, the forms of prayer, the difference prayer makes in the life of the believer, and why some prayers go unanswered. The leader's guide (#0-8358-0926-9) also offers suggestions on using the book for different time frames, such as six weeks, twelve weeks, or a weekend retreat.
#0-8358-0783-5

A Guide to Prayer for All Who Seek God by Rueben P. Job and Norman Shawchuck
For nearly twenty years, the beloved *Guide to Prayer* books have been sought after and used by thousands who hunger for God. Now, to the delight of many, compilers Rueben P. Job and Norman Shawchuck offer a third volume, *A Guide to Prayer for All Who Seek God*. It follows the Christian year and the lectionary readings. Each day offers guidance for an opening affirmation, prayer, and daily scripture selections. Job and Shawchuck also include spiritually grounded

explanations of the seasons of the church year to introduce each section of the book. This deluxe edition includes Bible binding, a ribbon bookmark, round corners, gold edges, and a leather-like cover in emerald green.
#0-8358-0999-4

Openings: A Daybook of Saints, Psalms, and Prayer by Larry James Peacock
Openings is a prayer book for every day of the year, especially written for people who don't think about using a daily prayer book. Peacock offers a devotional approach that encourages you to read a psalm or portion of a psalm each day and to reflect on life with God. He includes a wide variety of Christian prayer practices as well as prayers for peace, prayers of compassion, and seasonal prayers. Play and creativity, music, and physical movement in prayer are also part of the approach.
#0-8358-9850-4

Traveling the Prayer Paths of Jesus by John Indermark
In this six-week study, John Indermark invites us to walk with Jesus and to gain insights into prayer. We see that Jesus prayed at all times and in all places—for example, in the solitude of the desert and in the midst of crowds, on the mountaintop and in the garden. This beautifully written book opens us to grow in prayer.
#0-8358-9857-1

COMPANIONS ON THE WAY

Journeymen: A Spiritual Guide for Men (and for Women Who Want to Understand Them) by Kent Ira Groff
Bridging the gap between *Iron John* and the Promise Keepers, *Journeymen* encourages men to make the connection between being men and being Christian and provides a model for male spirituality by showing Christ as the true Mentor.
#0-8358-0862-9

Praying Together: Forming Prayer Ministries in Your Congregation by Martha Graybeal Rowlett
A summary of popular and effective prayer ministries used in local churches today. Twenty-one models are described including intercessory prayer chains, Taizé services, labyrinth walking, and Internet prayer, among others, to help church leaders start and develop their own prayer communities.
#0-8358-0979-X

The Workbook on Keeping Company with the Saints by Maxie Dunnam
Draw from the rich well of spiritual writing history as Dunnam guides you through the lives, teachings, and characters of William Law, Julian of Norwich, Brother Lawrence, and Teresa of

Ávila. Appropriate for individual or group use, this seven-week study contains questions for discussion, scripture, and reflection on the spiritual life.
#0-8358-0925-0

REACHING OUT IN LOVE

Yours Are the Hands of Christ: The Practice of Faith by James C. Howell
Many people are convinced that there is little observable difference in the lifestyles of Christians and non-Christians. Too often our spirituality seems invisible and mute to a hurting world. Christians long to make a difference in the world as a faithful response to the call of discipleship. *Yours Are the Hands of Christ* helps us find ways to express our faith actively in daily life and to make our commitment to Christ evident in today's world.
#0-8358-0867-X

Transforming Ventures: A Spiritual Guide for Volunteers in Mission by Jane Ives
With a strong emphasis on scripture, personal witness, and spiritual practices, this book provides for spiritual reflection and growth while people serve in short-term mission. Ives develops spiritual themes in mission and invites us to be open to God while we are away from home and when we return.
#0-8358-0910-2

Wrestling with Grace: A Spirituality for the Rough Edges of Daily Life by Robert Corin Morris
Morris encourages us to look at our first or reactive emotions—anger, frustration, sadness—in life's ordinary emergencies. Morris understands these reactive emotions as natural, and he persuades us to move beyond the reaction to cultivate a prayer of "the second breath." *Wrestling with Grace* is a "how to" manual about loving God, yourself, others, and the world around you.
#0-8358-0985-4

The Soul of Tomorrow's Church: Weaving Spiritual Practices in Ministry Together by Kent Ira Groff
Groff suggests that the soul of tomorrow's church will be restored as spiritual practices are woven throughout five ministry functions: worship, administration, education, soul care, and outreach. Every chapter teems with practical ways to weave spiritual practices of prayer, discernment, faith stories, silence, and hospitality in each one of the five specific ministry functions. *The Soul of Tomorrow's Church* brims with insights about crisis and ministry and offers practical solutions. The challenge for tomorrow's church is not to focus on new structures or programs, but to focus on ways to infuse ministry with new life.
#0-8358-0927-7

OTHER RESOURCES OF INTEREST

The Upper Room Dictionary of Christian Spiritual Formation by Keith Beasley-Topliffe
When you need practical information about spiritual formation, this book is an essential and basic source. Nearly five hundred articles cover the people, methods, and concepts associated with spiritual formation with a primary emphasis on prayer and other spiritual disciplines. #0-8358-0993-5

Alive Now
Alive Now seeks to nourish people who hunger for a sacred way of living in today's world. One of the most adaptable devotionals available, each bimonthly issue can be used as a daily devotional or simply read as a spiritual magazine. Included scripture follows both the themes presented and the church lectionary. With a mix of prayers, award-winning poetry, stories of personal experience, and contributions from well-known authors, *Alive Now* offers readers a fresh perspective on living faithfully. Also included is the "Taking it Further" segment that draws spiritual insights from books, films, and the Internet. Available as an individual subscription or group order.

Weavings: A Journal of the Christian Spiritual Life
Weavings is the award-winning journal for those who long to know God. Through thoughtful exploration of enduring spiritual life themes, *Weavings* offers trustworthy guidance on the journey to greater love for God and neighbor. *Weavings* readers have found that such guidance is enhanced when they read the journal with others through participation in small reading groups. These reading groups use *Weavings* articles as the framework for their conversation. Participants find that reading and responding to articles in the company of spiritual companions deepens their awareness of God's presence in their lives and in the world. We invite you to form a *Weavings* Reading Group and discover afresh that faithful friends are rare treasures (Ecclesiasticus 6:14). For more details on how to subscribe to *Weavings* and to download a free guide, *On Spiritual Reading*, which outlines how you might gather together a *Weavings* Reading Group, visit us at www.weavings.org. Or if you prefer, call 1-877-899-2780, ext. 7040, to request a guide.

The Upper Room Academy for Spiritual Formation
The Academy for Spiritual Formation cultivates spirituality with a balance of study and prayer, rest and exercise, solitude and relationships. The purpose of the Academy is to provide a place for committed individuals—clergy and lay— to experience God as part of an intentional Christian community. For more information, visit the Academy website at www.upperroom.org/academy, or call 1-877-899-2780, ext. 7233.

Notes

Preparatory Meeting

1. Thomas Merton, *Contemplative Prayer* (Garden City, N.Y.: Image Books, 1971), 37.
2. Elizabeth O'Connor, *Search for Silence* (Waco, Texas: Word Books, 1972), 21.

Week 1: Beginning the Journey

1. Nikos Kazantzakis, *The Saviors of God: Spiritual Exercises* (New York, N.Y.: Simon and Schuster, 1960), 54, 43, 51.
2. Saint Ignatius of Loyola as cited in *Dimensions of Prayer: Cultivating a Relationship with God* by Douglas V. Steere (Nashville, Tenn.: Upper Room Books, 1997), 2.

Week 3: Bread for the Journey

1. M. Robert Mulholland Jr., *Shaped by the Word: The Power of Scripture in Spiritual Formation*, rev. ed. (Nashville, Tenn.: Upper Room Books, 2000), 41.
2. Gregory the Great (540–604), *Moralia in Iob, Book 1*.
3. Example from Marjorie Thompson

Week 5: Companions on the Way

1. Timothy Jones, *Finding a Spiritual Friend: How Friends and Mentors Can Make Your Faith Grow* (Nashville, Tenn.: Upper Room Books, 1998), 19.
2. Ibid., 45.

Week 6: Reaching Out in Love

1. Henri J. M. Nouwen, *Making All Things New: An Invitation to the Spiritual Life* (San Francisco: Harper & Row, Publishers, 1981), 67.
2. Roberta C. Bondi, *To Love as God Loves: Conversations with the Early Church* (Philadelphia, Pa.: Fortress Press, 1987), 27.
3. George MacDonald, "Love Thy Neighbour," as cited in *Unspoken Sermons* (New York: George Routledge, 1873).

4. Mary Virginia Parrish, *No Stopping Place: Letters to My Grandchildren on the God I've Come to Know* (Franklin, Tenn.: Providence House Publishers, 2000), 59.

5. Keith Beasley-Topliffe, ed., *The Upper Room Dictionary of Christian Spiritual Formation* (Nashville, Tenn.: Upper Room Books, 2003), 99.

GLOSSARY

1. Keith Beasley-Topliffe, ed., *The Upper Room Dictionary of Christian Spiritual Formation* (Nashville, Tenn.: Upper Room Books, 2003), 44.

2. Ibid., 45.

3. Ibid., 67.

4. Ibid., 82.

5. Ibid., 99.

6. Ibid., 167.

7. Ibid., 167–68.

8. Ibid., 245.

9. Ibid.

10. Ibid., 254.

Evaluation

When your group has completed the *Exploring the Way* resource, share your insights and experiences. Copy this page if you prefer to keep it. Use additional paper if needed.

1. Describe your group's experience with *Exploring the Way: An Introduction to the Spiritual Journey*.

2. In what ways did the resource lead participants to a fuller understanding of spiritual formation and to a more experiential knowledge of spiritual practices? Please share your perceptions with us in this evaluation or through the discussion room at www.companionsinchrist.org.

3. What would improve *Exploring the Way*?

4. Do you have follow-up plans for your group? Do you plan to begin the twenty-eight-week *Companions in Christ* foundational course?

5. What other kinds of resources are you looking for? What other topics would you like to see in the Companions in Christ series?

Mail to: Companions in Christ
　　　c/o Robin Pippin, Editorial Director
　　　Upper Room Ministries
　　　P. O. Box 340004
　　　Nashville, TN 37203-0004
　　　or FAX: 615-340-7266

About the Authors

Marjorie J. Thompson is perhaps best known as the author of *Soul Feast*, a book on Christian spiritual practice that is widely used by individuals and groups. She has also written a book on the spiritual nurture of children in the home entitled *Family: The Forming Center* (Upper Room Books, 1996). Her articles have appeared in *Weavings, Worship, The Upper Room Disciplines*, and other publications.

Marjorie serves as Director of Pathways Center for Congregational Spirituality, a program position with Upper Room Ministries. She played a central role in the development of the core resource, *Companions in Christ*, and continues as Spiritual Director to the program.

Stephen D. Bryant is editor and publisher of Upper Room Ministries. His vision of small groups as important settings for spiritual formation and his experience in the contemplative life as well as local churches provided the inspiration for the Companions in Christ series. Stephen was instrumental in shaping the foundational twenty-eight-week *Companions* resource and continues to shape and cowrite the subsequent resources in the series.

Prayers for Our EXPLORING *the Way* Group

We sign this card to indicate our desire to be *lifted in prayer* and to add our group's name to the listing on the website as we continue our *Companions in Christ* journey. This ministry of prayer for *Exploring the Way* groups is an offering of The Upper Room Living Prayer Center and its numerous covenant prayer groups across the country. These prayer groups have made a covenant to lift us as individuals and as a group in prayer once our card is received.

Leader Name: _____ Leader Email: _____

Church Name: _____

Church Address: _____

Fold here and tape. — . —

City/State/Zip: _____

Church Email: _____

All members are invited to sign their first name below.

For information about *Companions in Christ* visit

www.companionsinchrist.org

Please include your return address:

_____

_____

_____

BUSINESS REPLY MAIL
FIRST-CLASS MAIL PERMIT NO. 1540 NASHVILLE TN

POSTAGE WILL BE PAID BY ADDRESSEE

UPPER ROOM MINISTRIES
PO BOX 340012
NASHVILLE, TN 37203-9540